A WALK ON THE BEACH

BROADWAY BOOKS / *New York*

A WALK ON THE BEACH

TALES OF WISDOM FROM
AN UNCONVENTIONAL WOMAN

JOAN ANDERSON

First edition published 2004

Photograph of Joan Erikson on page xiv courtesy of Matthew Cavanaugh.

Excerpt from "Slowly, Slowly Wisdom Gathers" from *That Shining Place: New Poems* by Mark Van Doren. Copyright © 1969 by Mark Van Doren. Reprinted by permission of Hill and Wang, a division of Farrar, Straus and Giroux, LLC.

Book design by Gretchen Achilles

Library of Congress Cataloging-in-Publication Data
Anderson, Joan, 1943–
      A walk on the beach : tales of wisdom from an unconventional woman / Joan Anderson.— 1st ed.
          p.   cm.
      1. Anderson, Joan, 1943–   2. Erikson, Joan M. (Joan Mowat)
      3. Women—Massachusetts—Cape Cod—Biography.   4. Middle aged women—Conduct of life.   5. Aged women—Conduct of life.
      6. Self-realization.   7. Cape Cod (Mass.)—Biography.   I. Title.
CT275.A7194A3 2004
974.4'92043'092—dc22
                                                                                          2003064943

ISBN 0-7679-1474-0

5   7   9   10   8   6   4

They are not dead who live in lives they leave behind—
in those whom they have blessed, they live again.

—MAYA ANGELOU

CONTENTS

PROLOGUE

Not a day goes by that I don't take a walk on the beach. The beach is truly home, its broad expanse of sand as welcoming as a mother's open arms. What's more, this landscape, which extends as far as the eye can see, always reminds me of possibility. It is here I can listen to my inner voice, shed inhibitions, move to the rhythm of the waves, and ask the universe unanswerable questions. That is why when I found myself at a crossroads in my marriage and my life, I ran away to Cape Cod and spent a year by the sea. I was sure this place, so full of my personal history, would offer clarity.

There is no more doubt that the sea is in my veins than that there is sand in my shoes. It was here where I spent my childhood summers; where I became engaged to my husband; where we returned after a three-year stint in the Peace Corps to await the birth of our first child; and where our children and their children now muck about during their summer vacation.

The beach to me is a sacred zone between the earth and the sea, one of those in-between places where transitions can be experienced—where endings can be mourned and beginnings birthed. A walk along the beach offers the gift of the unexpected. Scan the horizon and glimpse the endless possibilities. Stroll head down and encounter one natural treasure after another. Tease the tides and feel a sense of adventure. Dive into the surf and experience the rush of risk.

One of the most significant gifts the beach has given me was Joan Erikson, an elderly woman whom I met accidentally on a foggy February day. She was to prod me to find myself again, even when I thought all was lost.

It was intriguing to stumble upon someone so old and frail on such a dismal day—someone who, from the moment I laid eyes on her, became a source of fascination. Without knowing it, I had found the mentor I had been in search of—someone who would take me under her wing and help me understand what really matters. I was fifty-one, and she was some forty years my senior. She had retreated to Cape Cod to care for her ailing husband while I had run away from mine in order to recapture my original self. We became companions, prodding each other along to bigger and better things. A blithe spirit, she was always moving and difficult to catch. "Deep in the heart of me, find the best part of me," Joan wrote in one of her poems, and so for several years I chased after her uncomplicated wisdom in hopes that some of it would rub off.

Joan turned out to be the wife and collaborator of Erik Erikson, a leading psychoanalyst whose stages of human development deeply influenced the field of contemporary psychology. There I was, in a midlife crisis, when I met the person whose husband coined the term "identity crisis"!

The international lifestyle she led, the work she shared with her husband, her personal journey through the world of modern dance, the writing of five books, her discovery of the impact of art therapy as a tool in psychoanalysis, and her experience as a wife and mother offered me all the wisdom I needed to embark on the second half of my life. But what most fascinated me was that it was the adversity she experienced in childhood, not her charmed later life, that was most responsible for her attitude and ideals. "I started out making a billion mistakes, which turned out to be fertile ground for learning. Still, I get plowed under from time to time—perhaps I'm just a mess of weeds," she once told me, always irreverent and often self-deprecating.

Original people like Joan strive to deviate from the familiar path. They crave to know the unknown and seek challenges that most of us would avoid. From the minute we met, her creative approach to life kept me close to her side. Joan undertook to offer me some "Eriksonian actuality": she would strive to get me out of my head and into my body, make me more active than passive, teach me to lean on my senses and feel the intensity of experience, and not be "sooo serious." "Learning from life is much more beneficial than learning from a book," she said. "If given a choice, I almost always would stand up and shout."

And shout she did. She was once a feisty child, and her life story is a testimony to her insistence that "we should all plan secretly to get away from dependence as soon as possible. Learn any skill that opens up the world and sets you free."

When she was in her early twenties, she took off for Europe to research its dance schools, a trip unheard of for a single woman in the 1920s. "I was twenty and in a hurry—so eager for action, any action. I was a dancer and not interested in anything that would settle me down. I was looking for doors to open." But alas, she eventually met her soul mate and lover, Erik Erikson, an artist-turned-analyst who was studying with Sigmund Freud, and had two of their three children before they even married!

As a modern dancer with Isadora Duncan, she wore as little as possible, and as a faculty wife at Harvard, she rejected the proper tweeds for smocks, leotards, and short-cropped hair. "It's all about taking a stand when it really matters," she would say, "then living up to what you've gotten hold of and not letting it melt."

"I can't really remember my own midlife voyage," she said. "Perhaps I was spared the dreariness so many women find around this time because I had a job which challenged every creative impulse in my body. It was the kind of work that fed on itself and, in turn, made my life exciting. As I look back, this is when I should have had my depression but I just never got around to it. But then, I must confess that I don't enjoy depression very much. When I do hit bottom I try to figure out, as quickly as possible, how to get out of it."

Joan always offered action rather than advice. "The important thing is to *do* something, even if it's as simple as making a pile of pebbles. For it is always the doing that leads to the becoming, and before you know it you're on to the next stage of life."

In this book I have sought to capture the essence of our friendship and to impart some of the wisdom she shared with me. It is not a chronologically balanced account of our time together. As with any relationship, ours experienced spurts and lulls. During those lulls, we continued to spend time together and deepen our intimacy, but

5

for the sake of the story, I have focused on those periods when her inspiration was the most intense.

Her philosophy, if you could call it that, went something like this:

Welcome each day like a good meal.

The essence of a life well digested comes from knowing your strengths, overdosing on the senses, and remaining active and playful.

Keep your hands on the plow—push—don't ever stop pushing.

Always be willing to give a little more energy—the tension should always be there.

Then your life will never go limp.

My hope is that in the reading of this little book you will be mentored by Joan as I was. "The important thing is to share what you know," she said, time and again. "Be generative and pass it on. That is what makes all the difference."

CHAPTER ONE

OUT OF THE FOG

The call came as I was dressing to go out for dinner.
"Joan's dying," her caretaker announced without
preamble.

"What?" I was stunned and held the phone in silence
as my heart began pumping. "How could that possibly be?"
I asked, trying to push away the stark finality of Karen's
statement. "She was perfectly fine just a week ago, and so
full of herself at her birthday party." I could hear my voice
pleading.

"I know," Karen continued, "but sometime last week
she took to bed, her will broken somehow. These last few
months have been such a struggle. She so detested the
nursing home."

That was an understatement. Joan once told me that
she thought putting an elder in a nursing home was a bit
like taking the person to the dump. "The facilities are usually so far out of town," she said, "and the poor inmates are
estranged from everything real about life." But as her faint-

7

ing spells and frailty increased, her family and doctors felt that she needed the supervision, especially since she had a habit of firing the nurses hired to watch over her at home. Ever since she had been moved, though, I had watched her energy and determination slowly fade.

"Is she allowed visitors?" I asked.

"Yes, you could go over now, if you like. The family is having dinner."

I hung up the phone and sank into a nearby chair. A routine day had suddenly taken on immense implications. For the past several years Joan had been my mainstay. Although in many ways she appeared to be the antithesis of me—tall, patrician, at home in her body, overflowing with thought-provoking ideals—we quickly saw that we were both seekers. She was searching for ways to stay involved and vital until the end, and I, to depart from a structured life and all the roles I had been playing.

When Joan first appeared, I was in dire need of someone to help me jump-start my staid life, and she was the perfect coach. I had always gravitated to older people, especially those who distinguished themselves. Joan was wise, a bohemian by nature, who had routinely defied society's rules. Even more important, she made it clear that whatever we did together, we were going to have fun.

Since she was full of surprises, I suppose I shouldn't have been shocked that she would depart from this world without warning. Still, to hear that her death was imminent was too much to grasp. I needed to get to her bedside and see for myself.

Stifling my tears, I grabbed my car keys and drove off, harboring the hope that Karen was simply being dramatic and that Joan would soon be returning to her puckish self. The fifteen-minute drive passed quickly as visions flooded my mind—Joan at the beach, plopping seaweed on top of her head to look like a mermaid; Joan dancing around my kitchen on a cold winter's evening to the Beatles' "Hard Day's Night"; Joan riding in the back of a pickup truck, holding on tight while we skidded through thick sand on the way to the tip of North Beach.

I pulled into Brewster Manor's parking lot and headed for the nurse's station. At her own home, Joan would greet me on her deck, waving with both arms extended in a grand gesture. But away from her beloved small-town sounds—clanging church bells, chirping birds, and neighborhood children at play—her enthusiasm for grand salutations had waned.

I made my way down the antiseptic hallway, dreary on most days but especially cheerless in the evening, and as

I turned the corner, I saw a nurse exiting her room. "Is she . . ." I stumbled over my words, not wanting to suggest the worst.

"She's resting comfortably," the nurse assured me. "You may go in." I pried open the door and was greeted by a gentle breeze. Soft Celtic music played on a radio and the mesh curtains moved gently with the summer air. The walls were covered with pictures of friends, all of whom had only recently come to celebrate her ninety-fifth birthday. There was Joan, small frame tucked beneath crisp white sheets, her shrunken body so still, eyes welded shut. It was strange to see her so still. She had inspired me so—breathed life into me, as the Latin root says. How I yearned to be able to do that for her now.

I inched closer and sank down on the edge of the bed, not sure what to do next. "It's all in the touch," she used to say. "That's where you find the most in life." So I took hold of her paper-thin hand, gently rubbed her wrist and arm, and whispered, "I love you. Joanie, can you hear me? It's me. I'm here and I love you so very, very much." I paused after a few moments, hoping for some indication that she was aware of my presence—a wink, a nod, a squeezing of my hand would do, but nothing came. Nevertheless, as I gazed at the flickering candle on her bedside table, I couldn't help but smile, thinking back to our acci-

10

dental meeting and realizing that from the beginning, her flame had lit the way.

It was a dank, eerie February afternoon. The white world left behind by last week's snowstorm had turned to gray mush as the Gulf Stream blew its warm breath over the land. Even my hearty shell path was washing away as the piles of snow turned to water. I had been marooned in my little summer cottage all week with too many empty hours to dwell on feeling sorry for myself. My father was dead, my mother was losing her mind, my husband had started a new job far away, my sons were grown and gone, and where was I? A woman adrift—with unhealed wounds to prove it—a body forsaken, most daily functions given over to others, and a will detoured. I had retreated to Cape Cod to find some answers. Alone, in a warm and forgiving setting, I was convinced that I could right myself. But months had gone by, and I was still at a crossroads. Did I want to stay married or not? Should I continue writing children's books or do something else? What was the meaning of my life? Was all this soul-searching simply an exercise in narcissism? The only clear thought I had was that I didn't want merely to age . . . I wanted to compile experiences, lots of them.

As I gazed out the window, I saw that the thaw had created a formless fog that obscured all but the closest landmarks, not unlike my unfocused life. I strained to hear some sound other than the dripping of icicles. Coming through behind the silence, I heard a foghorn. Its steady drone called me out of my torpor and into the outside world.

I donned a yellow slicker, hopped into the car, plowed through the slush, and followed the horn to the shore as if it were a mother calling me home. Once at the beach, I walked gingerly, barely able to see my hand in front of my face. The sound of the lapping surf beckoned me toward the water's edge and helped me get my bearings. Suddenly, I knew that my goal was the jetty, a huge arm of rocks that defined the harbor at the end of this beach.

In fifteen minutes or so, I scrambled up onto the mighty boulders and began stepping from one to the next, intent on going all the way out to the invisible tip. Utterly alone, I felt a wild abandon and realized that I was enjoy-ing the solitariness of my adventure as much as anything else. But then I took a few more steps and found myself inches away from the chiseled profile of an old woman. She stood tall, a black cape flowing behind her, and looked out beyond the rocks almost as if she were a figurehead on the bow of a boat. It took me a minute or two to decide if she was real; then she turned her sparkling blue eyes on me. "Well, hello there. Are we the only ones in this town in a fog?" she quipped.

I chuckled at her play on words. "I hadn't thought of it that way. How do you do," I said, extending my hand. "I'm Joan Anderson."

"Really," she replied. "How curious. I'm Joan as well!"

I was still startled by her presence and momentarily at a loss for words.

"I just moved here," she continued, filling in the void. "Wonderful town, isn't it? I can't get enough of this beach."

"Where did you move from?"

"Cambridge," she said. "And you?"

"We have a summer cottage at the edge of town," I replied. "It's my first winter here."

"Are you living alone?" she asked.

"Yes." And then I surprised myself by continuing. "It's been quite a challenge being solo after a lifetime of living with a husband."

"Where is he?" she asked. I hadn't intended to spill out my story to a stranger, but my own honesty had prompted her question, so I attempted an answer.

"On Long Island. He took a new job and I decided not to go with him." I had never recounted that momentous decision quite so succinctly and was relieved to be met with a warm smile. As if sensing my embarrassment, she began to move.

"Would you care to join me?" she asked, even though I was already following her. Waves spilled over the tops of the rocks as we tiptoed around the slippery seaweed and puddles. Joan sped ahead with an agility that left me dumbfounded. How does she manage, I wondered. She must be eighty-five at least. "How come you're so nimble?" I asked out loud.

"Dance, my dear . . . it's been my passion forever."

"Do you still dance?"

"Whenever I get the chance," she said with a back-ward glance, as she extended one arm and pirouetted on her toes like a ballerina. Although I noticed that she grasped a gnarly cane, it seemed like a prop and simply added to her extraordinary gracefulness.

"What brought you out here on a afternoon like this?" I asked, my curiosity getting the best of me.

"Oh, I don't know. I suppose I was drawn to the gray-ness of the day," she said. "The mist sort of wraps around my thoughts and allows them to take hold. And you? What are you doing here?"

"Cabin fever," I replied somewhat more mundanely. "Last week's storm held me captive. My cottage is at the end of a very long road and there was no one to plow me out." Since she didn't respond to my explanation, I felt compelled to elaborate. "I feel a bit like that little boat smacking against the jetty," I continued, pointing one out a few feet away.

For a moment she stopped and let me catch up to her.

"How's that?" she asked.

"Oh, I don't know. I suppose I feel loosened, even free, now that I've eliminated all the responsibilities of my former life. But unfortunately, I also feel at sea, left without an oar or any idea of where I'm meant to row." Why was I babbling on—chatting so intimately to a virtual stranger?

"Funny you should describe your situation that way, dear, because I'm at sea as well," she admitted.

"You are?" I answered. "How so?"

"My husband isn't well," she said, all melody draining out of her voice. "I couldn't manage the two of us on my own any longer. Now that I'm here, we'll see what happens."

"Did you move him into a facility of some sort?"

"Oh, yes, a little nursing home in town," she said, pulling herself up and glaring out into the nothingness as if to defy a sense of resignation.

"How is it working?" I inquired cautiously.

"Nicely enough. A small town makes all the difference.

But most importantly, I was able to buy a house just up the street," she said with a chuckle, utterly delighted with her accomplishment. "I detest being confined, especially in a place with schedules and rules."

I was impressed. How did someone her age manage to rearrange her life so well? I was barely coping and I had only myself to think about. Before I could ask another question, she turned and squinted as if she had caught sight of something off in the distance. "It's important to always look out, not back," she said in a faraway voice. "I've left lots of luggage onshore, hoping I'll find some new things out here."

"The fishermen think like that," I said. "They go out, day after day, trusting the voyage and casting their nets on a whim. They always seem to come up with something."

"I'm not surprised." She nodded. "As far as I'm concerned vital living is all about action and touch. That's where you find the wisdom—in what you're doing and feeling. Steping out on a gray day, immersing oneself in the elements, daring to be different, that's the way to go. Thank goodness, there's no one as foolish as us right now. We can be in a fog all by ourselves!" And with that, she dropped her hood to let the air blow through her hair, increased her pace, and seemed intent on skipping the rest of the way.

"Sometimes I think women are like the fog."

"How do you mean?" she asked, stopping on a dime and turning toward me.

"We have a knowledge of what is underneath, but our real selves are obscured by what others think of us."

"Well, I suppose that's so. The mysterious female," she said with a hint of drama in her voice. "We'd best keep it that way."

I laughed at her gentle feminism. "I've been out here a hundred times and have never come across the likes of you." I stepped ahead and extended a hand to help her across the gaps in the rocks.

"It's all right, Mommy," she said, rejecting my help. "This old body hasn't failed me yet."

Eventually we arrived at the tip of the jetty and leaned against the base of the channel marker, yielding now to the wildness. As the bell clanged with the shifting wind, a gray-and-white gull swooped in and circled around us several times, flying so close we could see the intricate pattern of its feathers wrapped around its delicate cartilage. "What a beautiful creature," she exclaimed. "I bet it feels free, just like us right now."

"That's why I come here. It's a great place just to be and to think," I said, recalling the many times I'd sought out this place in the past couple of months, always leaving feeling uplifted somehow.

"There's more to life than thinking," she said gently, not meaning to contradict but wanting to make a point. "Everyone is soooo serious, don't you think?"

I fell silent and felt sad, even a bit guilty, about my tendency to see the dark side of things rather than gravitating to the light. Here she was at the end of her life with a sick husband and she was reveling in being selfish and silly. I didn't share her optimism, yet I was intrigued. I tried to recall a more lighthearted time so that I could stay on her wavelength.

"I've spent many summer days fishing with my boys on this jetty," I said. "In August, schools of snapper blues get caught in the incoming tide. You can't cast your line fast enough."

"It must be nice to have some history in one place," she said, sounding wistful. "I've always been a bit of a nomad—spent a good part of my early life running away."

"Perhaps I should have done the same," I said. "Then I wouldn't have had to run away from home at this stage of my life."

"I like you," she said, then changing the subject, asked, "What do you do, anyway?"

"I write children's books. Before that, I was a journalist. But I must confess recently I've been trying to journal my way through this crossroads I find myself at. So far my mind remains muddled and clarity eludes me."

"Give it time," she answered. "We all have original thoughts. It's just a matter of harnessing them."

"Well, you certainly seem to have a lot of them—original thoughts, that is. Would you happen to be a writer?"

"As a matter of fact, I've been writing a good part of my life," she quickly replied, as if she were eager to be found out. "It helps me to see through the muck and to figure out the answers to my own problems. No point in taking someone else's advice. What do they know of my experience?"

"I should think you'd have figured out most things by now," I said. "What keeps you going?"

"I was a wild child," she said, sounding devilish, "never did get tamed. My mother thought I was incorrigible. She called me bad, beautiful, and selfish. I suppose after hearing those labels enough, I was determined to live up to them. In a culture that is tight and mean about play, I've just pushed on, doing as I pleased."

"And now?" I wanted to hear that eventually she had straightened out and become sensible, as I had made myself behave for so many years.

"From the beginning I would say to myself, not there, not me. I knew what satisfied me and what didn't, what was real and natural for me. Normal is natural and natural is wild. I suppose that's why I love it out here," she said, leaning her head back while taking a few huge whiffs of salty air before gathering her cape about her as if she were suddenly chilled. "I've never been able to substitute words for experience," she continued. "You've just got to get out and embrace things." She reached over and took my gloved hand in hers, an intimate gesture for someone so new in my life, and indicated it was time to go. We walked back toward shore in silence, both of us perhaps reflecting on the good fortune of running into each other.

"I'd be delighted if we could meet again," she said as we neared the parking lot.

"I'd like that too," I said. "Can I give you a lift?"

"Thanks, dear, but I've arranged for a taxi to pick me up. He should be here any minute now. I detest not having a car and being dependent on others to get me around. I'm considering buying a golf cart, or perhaps a three-wheeled bicycle."

Her cab arrived and I opened the door. "Your last name—tell me how I can find you," I asked as she ducked gracefully into the backseat. "Erikson," she answered. "Joan Erikson. I live up Bank Street on Parallel. Call me, will you, dear?" And with that the door slammed and she drove off into the fog.

Had I just experienced an apparition or was this old woman the real thing? I suppose I wouldn't have an answer to that question unless she actually reappeared. I drove home in wonder.

CHAPTER TWO

KINDRED SPIRITS

It is only a week later that Joan calls to invite me to her home for an afternoon of port and conversation. "Bring some of your books along," she urges, "so we can share stories."

"But all I have are my children's books," I tell her, "nothing terribly intellectual."

"As far as I'm concerned children have all the wisdom anyway. I'll be intrigued, I'm sure."

In the days leading up to that first get-together I am full of both anxiety and expectation. I want to impress the magical lady I met at the beach, to keep her interest and prolong our conversation. Her house is set back from the road, tucked among towering oaks with birdhouses and feeders dangling from their branches and patches of perennial gardens everywhere. I all but stumble over a giant statue of Saint Francis, who calmly surveys the jumble as small birds peep uncontrollably. As I approach the back door, I see a small bell dangling from a cord with a sign attached: Ring Vigorously. I do just that, but to no avail. After knocking a few times, I peer into the window and there spot Joan, working out on a treadmill, dressed in a long black skirt and singing away as she treks. She waves quickly, slows down her machine, and hops off to open the door.

"Oh, my dear, it's so good to see you," she says, giving me a generous hug and planting a kiss on both cheeks. "Come in. Come in," she urges, taking my hand and leading me into a rather large entryway where a laughing brass Buddha peers down from a shelf high above.

"Well, I never expected to find you on a treadmill!" I say, taking off my coat and draping it over a nearby banister. "Is this typically part of your day?"

"When I'm left to wait for someone, instead of sitting around and peering out the window, I usually make use of the time with exercise. My body's my strength, you know. I've got to keep it in shape." She smoothes out her long sweater so that it hugs her slim hips and then tosses on a patchwork jacket that adds a dash of color to her ensemble. Just then the phone rings. As she races off down the hall, she instructs me to make myself at home.

I take advantage of her disappearance to study the artifacts that fill her space. Near the door is an impressionistic watercolor of a hooded woman who appears to be some sort of goddess. An inscription penciled in across the bottom reads:

> *I have painted this Grand Bead Shaman for you, Joan. Shamans are healers, Seers and visionaries in commu-nication with the world of Gods and Spirits. Their bodies may be left behind while they fly to unearthly realms. They are poets and singers, dancers and creative artists . . . spiritual leaders with repositories of knowl-edge, special beings, sacred and masters of ecstasy. Deep thanks for your latest book,* The Universal Bead, *and its incredible content.*
>
> *Duetty*

Her latest book! Who is this Joan Erikson anyway, and how many books has she written? I feel my anxiety rise as I wonder just what she expects from a friendship with someone who, at the moment, is dull and unproductive. I notice a nice blown-up photograph of children happily at play in Africa. Perhaps she's been in Africa, as have I. That would give us some common ground. The only other vibrant color in the room comes from a large tapestry of an Indian goddess.

Her belongings seem to reflect a life lived here and abroad, while her arts-and-crafts decor reveal someone with good taste and an eye for design. What I find the most fascinating is a felt board upon which she has pinned numerous black-and-white pictures. There are all sorts of groupings, mostly of the same people at various ages and stages, obviously family members, at the beach, walking in the city, gathering around a dinner table. Joan and a handsome man figure prominently in many. They are almost always holding hands, I notice.

I make my way toward the sound of her voice, past a tiny room with a single bed, antique desk, and chair, through the kitchen, where open shelves display pottery, beeswax candles, and handblown glassware, and finally into the living room, where Joan sits in an easy chair, legs propped up on a hassock, head tipped back against a cushion, chatting merrily like a teenager.

This room seems to define her. Jutting out from a corner, angled for the sunlight that is sure to pour in through the picture window, is the centerpiece—a long rustic table that she uses as a desk. It is piled with papers that appear to be ongoing projects, not just bills and correspondence. On the wall just behind this table, I notice a *Time* magazine cover and I move closer to see what it is about. The very same distinguished man from the family photographs is on the cover! Erik Erikson, the caption reads. I remember his name from the psychology courses I've taken—he was right up there with Jung and Freud! He's the psychoanalyst whose "stages of human development" influenced the entire field of contemporary psychology.

I look back at Joan and listen all the more closely to her charming chatter, trying to glean more answers from her gibberings. "Of course, dear, I would be entranced ... it would be my pleasure ... Thanks for sending a car ... that should make it easy. Until then ... bye, bye ..." Joan and Erik Erikson living in little old Harwich! Amazing, yet possible, I decide as I quickly calculate the thirty-five or so years that have gone by since the *Time* cover. I sink into the only other seat in the room, a swivel chair beside her table, and sway back and forth, thinking of how intrigued I've always been by Erikson's life-cycle theories. His major bestseller, *Childhood and Society*, broke with Freud by proposing that biology and sexual identity were only part of one's development. One's identity, he believed, is also derived from one's history and how one faces and resolves the many "identity crises" with which one is bound to be confronted. I found his interest in the development of each person's unique identity so hopeful, especially compared to Jung and Freud, who seemed to dwell on one's mistakes rather than on one's abilities. He studied with Sigmund Freud in Vienna before immigrating to the States, where he went on to design and portray the eight fundamental stages of human development, which changed the course of psychiatry ever after.

Joan finishes the phone call and turns her attention fully to me. "Shall I pour us a drink?" she asks, already up and on the way to the kitchen. "Port supports the loosening-up process, don't you think?" she says with a naughty twinkle. "We haven't time for censorship of thought or feeling, dear. We've got a friendship to develop."

I find myself suddenly looking at her with different eyes, studying her mannerisms and eccentricities, attempting to fill in the blanks. Her grandness and zest for life, as well as her seemingly enormous self-esteem, must have been enhanced by her marriage to such a celebrated individual. Besides, if she was Erikson's wife, and he was a crusader for finding the self, he surely would have encouraged her to be the grand lady that she has obviously become.

She returns in no time with a tray holding two stained-glass goblets, a decanter of port, and several cheeses hastily arranged on a wooden plate. "Now then, we're all set," she says, pouring the port and eager to get down to business. "To us," she toasts, raising her glass and taking a sip before sitting back down. "Let the unknown be born. Let change occur."

"Indeed," I say, taking a big gulp, seizing upon her

words. "Speaking of unknown, I'm dying to ask you something."

"Why certainly, dear. Go ahead."

"Is Erik Erikson, the man up there on the wall, actually your husband?"

I felt her eye me thoughtfully. "He is indeed," she says, her smile gradually widening. "We've been married for over sixty years."

"It's all too much," I continue, babbling away, my voice rising to a high pitch as it does when I'm excited. The reporter in me wants to go crazy and fire away a million questions, but I hold back. "I'm in awe!" I gush, realizing that if anyone can point the way and get me back on track, this woman can.

"You needn't be, dear. He did the work that he was meant to do. There's a plan for everyone if you are open to it. Erik was a restless, itinerant painter of children's portraits who had been lured to Vienna to become a babysitter and teacher in the progressive school run by Anna Freud. Eventually he was able to study with her father, Sigmund, and that's how he became a psychoanalyst. Imagine that?" she says, giggling at the coincidence. "He was just feeling his way like the rest of us. But tell me, dear, what attracted you to his ideas?"

ers? What really matters, anyway? Should I stay ma

and if so, what will that be like? I know for cert

can't be what it was."

"Wow, you've got a big plate of st

cludes. "Don't be so hard on yourse

off the past. You've taken a ma

rather than hiding under

are afraid of losing th

many women be

love. Having

in the e

life

g ...wistful.

'...ut it seems from the little you've told me about yourself, you're starting to find your way."

"I don't know about that. I've been here for five months now and still haven't the answers I'd hoped to have."

"Such as?"

"Who am I if I'm not playing one of many roles? How do I start pleasing myself after years of only pleasing oth-

ried,

in that it

ff there," she con-

f. It takes time to rinse

or step in just coming here,

he covers, as many wives who

eir security do," she continues. "So

eve that feeling dependent is a part of

a husband can be such an alibi for a woman;

d she never lives her own life. I believe that a full

needs to be about self-cultivation. Let's see some of

your books," she suggests, abruptly changing the course of

our conversation. "That was work you were doing just for

yourself all along."

I feel momentarily embarrassed as I pull a stack of forty-eight-page photo-essay books out of my satchel, all easy reads—hardly the lofty literature that surrounds her. "I started out as a journalist," I tell her, trying to puff up my credentials. She reaches for *Twins on Toes*, a ballet book, and begins leafing through the pages, saying nothing but shaking her head in a way I fear is critical. "Beautiful photographs," she finally offers, "but classical dance is so constricting, don't you think? Those poor girls with their feet all bound up in those awful shoes, and the contortions they are made to put their bodies through."

"But I thought you were a dance aficionado," I say, caught off guard by her response.

"Modern dance. That's why I went to Europe when I was young. All the experimentation in dance was taking place overseas. My goal was to connect with Isadora Duncan. She was the rebel—departing dramatically from anything that smacked of classical dance."

I consider the women in my family—grandmothers, aunts, even my mother—who allowed themselves few personal dreams and acted on even fewer. How did she get the gumption? I wonder. "How old were you when you did this?" I ask. "Did you have some sort of plan?"

"Not really, and no support from family or Columbia University, where I was a teacher. It was quite a risk for a young woman back in the 1920s. Still, I was determined as hell to get my life going. I sold my car, borrowed some money from my brother, and got on a ship bound for Le Havre."

As she talks, I remember my husband's and my decision to join the Peace Corps and go to Africa. There was no question that the experience changed the course of our lives. It gave us a different perspective, and our value system shifted altogether. We had found encouragement somewhere to follow our dreams, and Africa served to reinforce our appetites for continued adventure.

"Were you leaving any suitors behind?" I ask, recalling that even in my generation getting a man was more important than having a significant profession.

"Nobody serious," she answers glibly. "I was looking for my world to open up, not to close down. Becoming romantically involved would have stopped things. I simply became the girl who took herself to Europe. I even gave myself a new name and pretended I was someone else altogether. Of course, I eventually met Erik at a masked ball in Vienna," she says, with that twinkle that seems to appear each time she mentions his name. "That's the magic of life. It happens in a way that challenges our plans. But now it's your turn to talk," she urges. "You haven't really told me much about your writing, and what you're currently working on. I've been rattling on far too long."

"But I'd much rather hear about you," I answer.

"Fair is fair," she insists. "Reciprocity is key, you know. You can take some of my books home if you like," she says, gesturing toward the bookcase. "They'll give you plenty of information about me."

What can I tell her about writing that she doesn't already know? Besides, the more I hear about her, the more I want to know.

"I'm not working on anything at the moment, so tell me what your latest project is. Your desk appears full of research." I've always trusted my ability to keep the conversation off myself, and despite her attempt to get me going, she seems eager to talk about her own work.

"The importance of play all the way through life and how we all need to unlearn the rules that are set up for us by others. That's one of the things I like about you. By taking yourself away, my dear, you have broken a major rule. Bravo!"

I look into her vibrant face and see the understanding I have yet to find from others. Indeed, this stranger is the first person actually to affirm my decision. Her approval makes me soar. "That's how I became my own person," she continues. "Even before I left for Europe I was always running away to the woods, playing hooky during the school years, seeing how much I could get away with. I was well aware of my place in the family—a third child and not particularly wanted. Most of my learning took place in my secret life."

"Come to think of it, because we moved so often, I

guess I was somewhat of a loner, too. I surely didn't get all the advantages that were offered to my older brother."

As we continue to share stories, we discover more that we have in common and our conversation bounces back and forth faster than a Ping-Pong ball, gradually breaking down the barriers of anonymity. In the past, I had quickly lost myself in the lives of others, often becoming what they demanded. But I sense that this friendship will be different. I suspect that Joan already has a sense of our potential friendship, and since I yearn to escape the narrow confines of my own existence, I am ripe for this new path. Already her childlike glee has begun to bring me back from the seriousness of my exile.

"It's getting late," I say, as the light begins to fade. She walks me to the door.

"It's been a glorious afternoon, dear," she says, holding both my cheeks in her hands, her blue eyes looking deeply into mine. "I'll see you again soon, right?"

"Absolutely. It's something when you find yourself at a dead end and then, voilà, someone pulls you out of the doldrums," I say, smiling broadly at my new friend.

"Kindred spirits. That's what we are," she says. "Just think, if you hadn't risked your marriage and come away, you'd just be another one of those summer people I pass in town."

I smile and head down her steps, looking back once to see her waving me off, with both arms held over her head. She certainly has ready access to depths of feelings and insights that I, up until now, have approached the long way around. I shake my head. Having foundered long enough, I sense my soul is finally about to set sail. In any case, my self-protection is beginning to unravel with the warmth and wisdom that comes from new friendship.

CHAPTER THREE

HOLY FOOLS

T ake me to all the places that entrance you," Joan half-beseeched, half-commanded during one of her frequent phone calls. She has taken to calling me at an extraordinarily early hour almost daily, eager for adventure and to explore this place that has offered her escape. Throughout the spring I have continued to comply since she fervently believes that learning from life is much more beneficial than learning from a book. "Activities become fertile ground for musing," she insists. During the past few months, we have scoured the beaches, trekked through the Provinceland dunes, climbed to the top of lighthouses and windmills. I even took her out to the flats to clam on one especially warm day. If I have difficulty coming up with a good idea she can always be counted upon to fill in the blanks and tempt me away from whatever I have planned.

"So what do you have on tap for today?" she asks on this hot June morning as I sip my coffee and let my foggy mind focus.

"What day is it, anyhow?" I ask.

"Saturday," she says cheerily.

"Oh, I have a wedding to go to," I answer.

"That sounds like fun. Can you get me invited?"

"I'm not attending as a guest," I remind her. "I'm the new wedding coordinator at the church, remember? I need to unlock the doors for the florist and wedding party and then be available for anything the wedding party might need."

"But you could you use some help, couldn't you?" She sounds like a child begging to be included. "I could arrange flowers, light the candles, and ease the groom's jitters. Men are always petrified, you know."

"Well, if you really want to," I acquiesce, but if truth be told, I am not certain whether she will be a help or a hindrance. "The wedding is at two. I'll be at the church by noon."

She is waiting on the steps, when I arrive, looking stunning in gray crepe and holding tightly to a broad-brimmed straw hat. In no time, the stark white sanctuary begins to feel like the stage of a theater on opening night. Florists are hanging from ladders draping boughs of wild flowers and ivy from the wall sconces; the janitor is re-arranging the altar furniture to make room for the rather large wedding party; Joan is placing baskets of flowers on the numerous windowsills; and I am wiring large satin bows on the end of every pew. Given the fragile state of my own marriage, I find it a bit ludicrous that I have taken on a job in which I help ease young people into a life they can't possibly imagine.

"Hey, Joanie, was there this kind of fuss for your wedding?" I call to her from across the sanctuary.

"Hardly," she chuckles. "Erik and I were married on April Fool's Day in Vienna. In the end family members who didn't get to attend made the only fuss. We had to have a Jewish ceremony to honor Erik's father's persuasion, and an Anglican ceremony to honor mine. Then of course there was the civil ceremony at the town hall, a law in Europe. It was a bit overdone . . . almost ridiculous!"

"Whatever works," I answer. "Maybe having three weddings kept your flame that much more alive."

"I don't know. It's all such a gamble. Who knows why one couple makes it and another fails? What was your wedding like?"

"A huge disappointment, actually. I had dreamed of a big pageant, but when I agreed to get married in Africa, all those plans had to go. My husband ended up coordinating most of it because he was already in Kampala. Even if he'd understood my girlish dreams, the community and environment didn't provide much in the way of flourish. We had only a handful of guests in a tiny chapel that was hardly glamorous—white gown but no glory. Plus I was panicked. I'd known him for only nine months. The flight to Uganda took forever and gave me too much time to agonize over what I was doing. I felt like a mail-order bride."

"Sounds like an adventure to me. I've always wanted to go to Africa."

"It was that, but also somewhat of a convenience for us . . . a way to earn a salary and therefore afford to be married. Amazing how we put so much trust in love," I add, "when really, we had no idea what we were getting into."

"Nobody ever does, dear," she says, while casually inserting daisies and ferns into the bows I've hung. "Marriage is at best a foolish endeavor, but well worth it, I have to say, if you're lucky enough to get hitched to a best friend."

"You think so?" I ask, intrigued by her candor.

"Oh my goodness, yes. That's why Erik and I call ourselves 'Holy Fools.'"

Just then the groom walks into the sanctuary with his best man and three handsome ushers. "How are you holding up, Tommy?" I ask.

"Not bad, not bad," he says, "but I can't manage to get my boutonniere to stay on."

"No problem," I say, stopping to pin a white rose and stephanotis to each man's lapel.

"A good twenty minutes before two, you'll want to re-tire to that room over there," I say, pointing to the sacristy. "It's bad luck to see your bride before the wedding, you know."

"Such a handsome young man," Joan whispers as we quickly tidy up the mess of floral boxes, candle wrappings, and odds and ends.

"Where do you get your energy?" I ask. "It's occurring to me that I couldn't possibly have finished this job with-out you."

"It's fun having a purpose, dear—keeps the adrenaline going. Being involved has gotten me through many a lull."

The soothing background music of a string quartet fills the sanctuary, and I suggest that after Joan unpacks the programs, she take a seat to relax and enjoy the moment while I await the bride's arrival. I tuck myself into a cor-ner of the vestibule and melt into the scene of friends, fin-ery, and flowers.

So many details go into a wedding . . . such commitment on so many people's parts to make sure that everything is just right. As the soloist begins a rendition of "O Perfect Love," I shake my head and find myself thinking that there is for sure no such thing as a perfect love. Perhaps a perfect wedding day, but even then, there are flaws. Actually, I've heard that the more flaws the better. If you can accept the imperfections of your wedding, you're better able to let the unfulfilled expectations of your life roll off your back.

Just then I see a confection of white beyond the stained-glass window. The bride, Sara, and her attendants are tiptoeing up the walkway. I close the chancel doors and suppress my hardened thoughts. The organist has begun to play some variations of Wagner's *Lohengrin*, and as I peek through the crack in the door, I see that the minister and groom are in place.

"All right then, here goes," I say as I throw open the doors to send one bridesmaid, then another down the aisle. "Are you ready?" I ask the bride as her eyes fill up. She nods, before planting a kiss on her father's cheek. There is a hush as all eyes strain to the back of the church. "It's time," I whisper to Sara as I straighten her train and urge her forward, then slip into a seat next to Joan as the minister's voice reaches out to the congregation: "Dearly Beloved, we are gathered here together to join this man and this woman . . ."

I gaze at several young couples across the aisle, some dewy-eyed, others with blank expressions, a few holding hands, and wonder about their relationships. Surely in this age of free love and unbinding commitment they've already had their fair share of heartbreak. It isn't easy deciding to get married these days. Before the pill, most of us jumped into marriage in order to jump into bed, but that isn't necessary anymore. In some ways, with so many choices, the commitment today's young people make is all the more impressive.

When I look up at the front of the church, I see Sara and Tom looking at each other in such a satisfied way: her face serene, his expression rapt. They are convinced that their love is strong enough to withstand everything. How do loving feelings diminish so when the intention, the commitment, and the love are so strong at the beginning? I can't imagine a soul in this church who isn't feeling awakened by the familiar lines of this service. The lucky ones feel grateful and affirmed that they are themselves joined to another, and some, no doubt, are quickened by regret and despair. Who among us can listen to the minister lead Tom and Sara through their vows without feeling the depth of this couple's aspirations? I can't help but think about how easy it is to pin our failed dreams on the next generation. Every wedding sparks the hope that the young people will get right whatever it is that has eluded us. "Wilt thou love her, comfort her, honor and keep her?" the minister asks Tom, who answers all too readily, "I will."

Love, honor, comfort—all bold ideals to which only the naïve and foolish can promise to adhere. What do I honor about my husband after thirty years, anyway? How often do I comfort him anymore? And what's worse, I can't even remember how long it has been since he comforted me.

Nonetheless, the ritual of the wedding ceremony draws me in. I forget my doubts and misgivings as the groom steps on his bride's long veil and pulls it to the floor; the best man fumbles in his pocket in search of the rings; and the bride nervously giggles and stumbles over her vows. All too quickly, it seems, the minister concludes, "Oh God, who has so consecrated the state of matrimony that in it is represented a spiritual marriage, look mercifully upon these servants, that their home be a haven of blessing and peace." And the official sounds of the service cease.

The bride and groom kiss as thunderous applause goes up from the congregation and they turn in triumph to recess past their gathered family and friends. In a mere twenty minutes, Sara's and Tommy's lives have been irretrievably changed, hopefully for better, perhaps for worse, but certainly forever.

"Seems as though the church bells should be ringing," Joan whispers as I was just thinking that such a moment of tangible transition could do with a bit more flourish. After the bridal party recesses, row upon row of guests file out until the sanctuary is completely empty again. "Phew!" I sigh, wiping my brow. "I'm completely undone. What did you think of all that, Joanie?"

"They seem to be a very sweet couple," she says in a wistful, faraway voice. "Earnest, I'd say, especially the groom. He was right there, giving in to the moment unabashedly. I love to see that in a man. Most of the time, they seem so bottled up that you haven't a clue as to what they're thinking much less feeling. A wedding ceremony is imbued with such hope, isn't it?"

"I remember being almost outside the moment when I got married," I muse, "going through the actions as if I were in a play, not really believing that something significant was happening. My husband seemed much more sincere and present."

"I recall thinking that it was all so silly. What was the fuss about anyway? Erik and I were stuck from the first kiss. We didn't really need all that folderol. Yet somehow, making promises in front of clergy and witnesses brings the whole thing to a holy level, don't you think?" Joan asks.

"I suppose it gives you something to hold on to when times are tough," I add.

"It's the reverence with which we exchange the wedding vows," she continues. "None of us can know what's ahead and worse still, we are all so ill equipped for so many of our struggles. It helps to be able to point back to the joy

44

and holiness of the wedding day, and then laugh a little at the absurdity of life and love. We can save any situation with lightness. That's where foolishness comes in," she says. "Keep playing the fool, that's my motto. It's the dreams that pull a couple together, and most dreams prove foolish in the face of reality, but we need to honor them anyway. That's what's holy about a relationship."

"Hmmmm, I've never thought about it that way," I say. "I tend to focus on how dreams so often get confused with expectations."

"Oh, my dear, you really get into a rut if you have too many of those," she says, her directness momentarily shocking me. "You end up aiming for the expectations in-stead of just living the life that comes to you—the foolish-ness helps you respect your dreams without getting too weighted down by them."

The custodian who is removing the bows from the pews and several guests who are carting off the flower baskets soon interrupt us. "I suppose we'd better begin to lock up," I say to Joan, standing up and straightening my wrinkled skirt.

"How about walking me over to Rosewood when we're done?" she asks. "I'd like for you to meet Erik."

"That would be lovely." I smile at the thought, both cu-rious and honored for such an opportunity.

"He doesn't speak," she warns me. "After his hip surgery he began to serenely retire. Stopped talking altogether. I suppose he feels that he has said all that he needs to for one lifetime."

"I should think so," I agree, marveling that her respect for him endures even though he is in decline.

The nursing home is a ten-minute walk up Main Street. Once we are inside, several nurses greet Joan with familiar hugs. "Erik's in the parlor," one of them informs her. Joan makes a beeline for the door, but not before greeting several wheelchair-bound patients along the way. Once at the door she scans the room. "There's my guy," she says, pointing to a handsome man gazing out the window, a spot of sunlight illumining his mop of thick white hair.

I hang back, not sure what to do next as she rushes to his side and pulls a chair up next to his. She puts her arms over his shoulders and clutches his left hand with hers; I am almost embarrassed to be witnessing such an intimate moment. Still, it is said that the light shed on a good relationship illuminates all relationships, and so I stare at her gestures for a clue about what it means to be permanently connected. Just then she reaches into her pocket for a piece of chocolate, unwraps the foil covering, and slips it into his mouth. They sit in silence for a few more minutes, when she suddenly remembers that she brought me along.

"So sorry, dear, I almost forgot you were here," she says, motioning for me to approach. "Come meet Erik." I ease myself forward, feeling humbled, knowing that she invites very few people to this place. "Erik, dear, this is my new friend, Joan. Isn't it fun? We have the same name." I extend my hand, and look into his eyes, but his gaze soon returns to his own Joan.

All along the intercom has been providing meaningless background music, until Joan hears the strains of "The Vienna Waltz."

"Our song," she says to Erik, her voice becoming both excited and melodic. She moves her chair even closer so that they face each other and takes his hands in hers, moving them to the tune as if their bodies are floating around some grand hall in Europe. I envy her freedom. She doesn't seem to have a care of embarrassing herself. She seems lost in a memory, perhaps recalling their meeting at a masked ball. I sense that I have intruded long enough and retreat to the garden, where I sink into a wicker chair and wilt in the muggy summer air.

I must have dozed off, for the next thing I know Joan is tapping me on the shoulder.

"Erik's napping," she says. "I usually wait until he awakens before going home. Would you care to stay awhile longer?"

"Sure. There's no one waiting for me at home."

"Well, we're kind of in the same boat then, wouldn't you say?"

"Hardly," I answer. "You have someone to whom you are devoted. I'm not sure I can say the same. Seeing you and Erik just now, still so connected after all these years, and earlier that sweet bride and groom, I must admit that I'm feeling a bit deflated."

"That's the trouble with these spectacles. They present a totally unrealistic picture of everything. People who live together for a long time inevitably disappoint and hurt as well as gratify and please each other. It's human nature. Then there are all the power struggles. You don't think for a moment that Erik and I have been perfect all the time, do you?"

"No, I suppose not."

"Love is a risk and divorce is reasonable," she says matter-of-factly.

"You really think so?" I ask, somewhat surprised that she would be so cavalier.

"Oh, indeed. One of my best friends was married to an absolute dud. She was better off when she got rid of him."

I wonder what denotes a "dud" in her mind. Certainly I've never thought of Robin as one. I guess I should be relieved about that.

"Look, dear, as I said earlier, marriage is holy, but it needs a light touch. You can't always focus on the relationship. You'll hardly be able to breathe. Besides, such devotion is a nuisance. I think you've probably given yourselves a necessary break. What sort of an arrangement do you have, anyway?"

Her question jolts me. I am temporarily speechless. "Actually we have no arrangement. I never entertained the idea of divorce or separation, for that matter. I just seemed to want a vacation from marriage. In the interim he has been clarifying his own issues and just lately he's been talking about early retirement and joining me here. So, to answer your question, we have no arrangement—just a loose thought that in time we will be back together again."

"I think you are quite brave," she says, startling me. "So many couples cling to what they had instead of moving on to what could be. You know, the poet Rilke had it right when he suggested that the highest task for two people in a relationship is to stand guard over the solitude of the other. Perhaps you and your husband are actually being more innovative than others."

"I hope you're right."

"Erik and I were pretty unpredictable," she continues. "We were always adjusting our life to whatever he was involved with at the moment. Sometimes he would work twenty-four hours at a time; other times he was home for days on end. You have to understand each other's situation and be on the same wavelength to put up with such fluctuations. But, thinking back on it, perhaps it was the unpredictability that helped us escape the weight of routine. I think our devotion to our routines causes us to lose sight of each other as separate individuals."

I continue to feel some consolation as she talks but I also need to change the subject. As we are still in the early stages of friendship, I am anxious to impress her with my life, not air quite so much of my dirty laundry. I glance over her shoulder and see a nurse pushing a wheelchair, bringing Erik out to the garden. Once again Joan gets that look—dazzled at the very sight of him. Three's company, I find myself thinking. Her time with him is of the essence. I take my leave, filled with bittersweet, conflicting thoughts.

CHAPTER FOUR

OVERDOSE ON THE SENSES

On the occasional Sunday I have introduced Joan to my favorite little Episcopal church, knowing that the familiar service would take her back to her Anglican roots and childhood in Gananoque, Canada. The chapel is nestled in a hollow and surrounded by tall protective pine trees. When all is quiet, I can hear the birds feeding at their various houses on the property, and beyond the candles and flowers, I can smell the sea that permeates the wood of this tiny sanctuary.

Everything in this place is handcrafted—the altar, the stained-glass windows, the hammered metal sconces with their dripping candles, the old sailing ships that hang from the rafters, and the baptismal font carved in the shape of a scallop shell. The entire church is an offering from the community. I can sense that their handiwork helped these seekers hone their beliefs.

By the end of today's service, I am completely at peace and ready to head home, but Joan seems to want to dawdle. She is wandering in the cemetery, around the old tombstones that are scattered under several magnificent oak trees. I have an aversion to cemeteries, so I'm half intimidated, half entranced, but I follow her, nonetheless, as she makes comments about the local inhabitants.

"Venerable names and very Yankee," she notes. "Did you happen to notice their life spans? Most of them were quite long-lived." She wanders on in a world of her own and eventually stops in front of a rather large, ornate piece of granite. *"Elijah Doane,"* she reads aloud. *"Beloved Husband, Father, Grandfather... 1860-1928.* Hmmm. You know," she says, turning her eyes on me. "It really doesn't matter how much time you have on this earth, as much as what you make of it."

"Excuse me?" I move closer to give her my undivided attention.

"It's all about that right there," she says, taking the point of her cane and laying it in between the dates, "how much you make of your dash. I was amused once to find a poem on this very idea." And then, she pulls herself upright and begins reciting something about the date of birth and the date of death, but the dash speaks for all the time one spends on earth. "Quite a concept, isn't it," she says while gazing back at the tombstone. "Obviously Mr. Doane was a family man. Who knows what else he did, but I can promise you, it's more than the dash reveals. Every time I visit a cemetery, I'm reminded to squeeze just a little more out of my day."

We continue to walk, up one row and down another, until Joan stops abruptly and looks straight at me. "How old are you, dear?"

"Fifty-one."

"That's all! You've only just arrived at the midpoint. I figure that if you're to make it to my age, you've got a good four hundred and eighty months left to go—lots of time left to spend your dash," she says, almost cackling over her eerie foresight.

"Four hundred months, is that all?" I sink into silence at the thought. Do I even remember what happened last month, or yesterday, for that matter?

"Let's move on from this churchyard and go have some brunch at my place," I offer, in an effort to change our course a bit.

"Sounds heavenly. I love your cottage and you do have a way with food, dear. Come to think of it, I'm starving." We walk arm in arm toward the car, pile in, open the windows, and let the breeze blow through our thoughts on the way home until Joan begins quoting from the Bible. *"Make us know the shortness of our life that we may gain wisdom of heart,"* she says. "That's from the Psalms. My father made us memorize half the Bible," she continues. "Some of the lines come in more handy than others."

I'm anxious to get back to the cottage and my cozy woods and away from death and dying. She's made me too aware of how little I take each day for granted, and it's upsetting me. Preparing breakfast will get me out of my head. Once in the kitchen, I forage around the refrigerator and pull out mushrooms, scallions, fresh basil, and some Gouda cheese, and then find a can of artichoke hearts. While the vegetables sauté, I put some music on the stereo and call to Joan, "Would you like a glass of port or a Bloody Mary?"

"A Bloody Mary sounds good," she answers. "I only have port in the late afternoon or before I have to give a speech."

I smile at her ability to confess a quirky habit and mix up the mildest of drinks, having come to learn that a little bit of alcohol goes a long way at her age and stage.

"What can I do to help, dear?" she asks.

"Why don't you set the table?" I suggest. "The place mats are in that drawer over there, and the silverware in a tray nearby." But Joan soon wanders off to the living room without touching the table. I find her eyeing a modern African painting. "We spent most of our spare money on art," I tell her. "It's been our passion since the beginning."

"From the looks of your books and pottery, it seems

you have many passions, dear," she says, holding an onyx sculpture of a man and woman intertwined. She leaves that thought hanging in the air, making me feel as though I should comment. Instead I start cracking eggs.

"Brunch is served," I announce a half hour later, and she promptly rushes to the table. "I'm famished," she says. "Church does that to me."

"Me too," I agree.

"It looks beautiful . . . all these good vegetables," she says while squeezing lemon into her drink and then taking a bite of cranberry bread. "I must confess, I rarely bother to fuss, living alone as I do—one of the bad habits of single life. What's that interesting music coming from the stereo?"

"The Paul Winter consort. Do you know his stuff?" She shrugs as if she doesn't recognize the name, more intent now on digging into her omelet.

"He's composed a whole series of work that celebrates the earth and he calls it living music."

"Well, this number sounds surreal," Joan observes, "otherworldly even. I love it when musicians push through to new sounds."

"It's called 'Canyon.' The musicians carried their instruments down into the depths of the Grand Canyon in order to capture the echo of the place. Can you imagine?"

"Amazing," she says, her eyes bulging as if she can picture such a trek. "Who would ever think of such a thing . . . going to such trouble to make music in a particular setting?" And then, after several more mouthfuls, she puts her fork down and closes her eyes, a sign that I have learned means she would like to be quiet and just experience the moment.

I follow suit, although I find it hard to take myself too far out of my kitchen. Nevertheless, we sit solemn for a good five minutes until I dare to peek out of one eye and sense that she is half asleep with the music beating her temples. Her face appears translucent, her breathing shallow, her body limp. Is she all right? I wonder. Has she had a spell? Was the drink too strong? As the music crescendos and then grows soft, Joan emerges from her trance, and I see that her eyes are brimming with emotion. "Wow! I've been gliding with the ravens, soaring above the mesas, dipping down into crevices. It brings me back to one of my most sensational trips."

"Oh yeah?"

"We were in Zion National Park with signs pointing every which way to trails. My brother, sister, and mother had no interest in rock climbing, but I did. I took off like a mountain goat and ended up on top of a red and yellow world of rock where eagles soared, shrubs oozed with smell, and the air was intoxicating. I was drunk with weariness and satisfaction. That's kind of how I feel right now—like I've climbed into the canyon and then back out again." She takes one more swallow of her drink and rises from her chair. "The music makes me want to get up and out," she says. "How about showing me that pond of yours?"

"Good idea," I agree, shaking my head at her indefatigable enthusiasm and thirst for adventure. We promptly dump the dishes in the sink, grab sunglasses, and head out toward the path that leads to the pond. Joan walks ahead of me, bouncing on the pine needles and moss as we make our way through the tunnel of balsams.

"A summer day is always an invitation to wander off, don't you think, dear?" I nod as she skips off, reminding me of my children when they were little. The boys named this place the Enchanted Forest, and they would dawdle, just as Joan is, looking for ladybugs, collecting toadstools, finding sticks that could be made into swords or saved for marshmallow roasts. Like them, Joan seems delighted that her ankles are getting wet from the thick growth of newly sprouting fern, and even more excited when she hears an oriole. "I haven't heard an oriole sing for a very long time," she says, craning her neck to find the source of the sound.

"It's hopeless to spot any creatures in this mass of

trees," I say, impatient and wanting her to hurry along. "C'mon, we have another quarter of a mile to go." Just as we pick up our pace, a stream of light pushes through the opening of a stand of pines, its ray creating a spotlight on a majestic doe, all beige and white, nibbling away at bark. We freeze, unable to believe we are so close to such a wild thing. She glances over at us, gives off a little huff, flicks her white tail, and then bounds gracefully into a thicket.

"Animals go about their lives despite us, don't they?" Joan whispers, still transfixed. "They demand nothing of us humans, really."

"Too bad it doesn't work the other way around," I say.

"How do you mean?"

"The ecosystem. Animal life is basically responsible for the balance of everything, and yet most people don't see it that way. I once did a children's book called *Earthkeepers* that focused on ecology."

"What a lovely title, dear. We should all aspire to such a role."

"No kidding. One of the 'earth keepers' was a man in the wilderness of Minnesota studying the lifestyle of bears. He figured that one bear needed about a half acre of trees in which to feed himself. Developers in the area wanted the trees cut down for resorts and leisure housing. My earth keeper friend was trying to make them understand that as the trees go, so do hundreds of species that also live in that half acre, unseen of course, but still vital, contributing to the ecology of that particular space."

"It makes sense," Joan answers. "So what happened?"

"What do you think? The developers won. That's why the bears are encroaching on camps, foraging for food, and moving closer to cities. Everything is not as it should be."

"Hmmm," she utters. We walk on in silence, I in the lead now, she stopping on occasion to turn one thing or another over with the tip of her cane. "Quite a few mush-rooms in your woods," she says, entranced with a giant or-ange-and-white one. "I used to collect them when I was little . . . had a book that explained every imaginable vari-ety." She moves off the path toward a clump of toadstools. "Here's a deadly amanita," she exclaims, cackling like a witch doctor. "You eat one of these and that's it."

A mosquito bites my leg and I give it a good whack as I feel my impatience returning. "C'mon, Joanie, let me help you down," I say, extending my hand and motioning to her. We inch our way down the path, which is more liquid than solid, and finally step safely onto the sandy shore. "Here it is," I boast, presenting her with the open space and a circular body of fresh water. "What do you think?"

"Wow. A pond is so serene and safe, wouldn't you say? So different from the ocean."

"Well, for one thing, it's a contained body of water," I offer. "I always feel a sense of contentment—of being held—I suppose because you can contemplate swimming from one side to the other side."

"Shall we," she asks, jokingly. Just then she catches sight of a windward feather blowing along the shoreline, taking flight, and Joan can't resist trailing after it, losing the feather but continuing on toward a float, which sits on the edge of the shore.

"Whew! That was quite a jaunt," she says, motioning for me to follow. Joan eagerly slips out of her shoes and starts to swing her feet in and out of the water, working up to a splash the way little children do just after their mothers have warned them not to get wet.

"I'm home," she says gleefully, "totally at home."

"Growing up in Ontario, I guess you felt pretty land-locked," I say, sitting down beside her now and joining in the fun.

"Except for a lake we went to every summer, I rarely ever got to see water. At the lake there was a little cove tucked in between two rivers. To get there involved slipping and sliding down a grassy hill, crossing a small brook, and then running through Miss Macker's woods. I felt so safe there—cozy with rocks on both sides of a tiny bare space. It drew me in like a magnet with its gentle force, purpose, and eagerness. Lapping water against rocks—swishes along the beach were like heartbeats marking time and making all previous jars of the day remote. Magic . . . the whole place was magic."

She is eyeing a rowboat not ten feet away. "I wonder if the owners have left the oars," she asks, abruptly changing the subject and teasing me to go find out. I mosey over, half hoping they haven't. But alas, they are stowed neatly inside. "Are we in luck?" she asks.

I nod reluctantly.

"It's been a while since I've rowed," I warn her. "My seafaring craft is a kayak. But hop in. No harm in trying. We can't get lost, that's for sure." Joan has gotten herself off the float and into the boat before I can finish my thought. I secure the oars in their locks, and with a big push shove off, then jump quickly aboard.

"Neatly done, dear," she says, and then turns her body as if she were the coxswain, ready to call the orders for a race. A snapping turtle that has been sitting on a nearby dock plops into the water and follows us. In the distance, I see lake bass leap up from beneath the surface. The oars are heavy compared to my kayak paddle, but I adjust and find my rhythm—their hollow creak as they rub against the locks creates the only unnatural sound around the pond.

"The great joy is when something happens serendipitously," Joan says, "like an unexpected breeze, or finding this boat. I never feel as though I am living unless I am making contact with the world like we're doing now. In my youth, I would walk the streets of New York and smell the neighborhoods, all the aromas of people from other places, or walk across the great bridges with rain-soaked hair and the wind on my skin, or go to museums where I would get so close to a painting that I could smell the oil. Do you know what I mean, dear?" she asks, extending her hand now over the edge of the boat and letting the water race through her fingers. "We're taught early on to stop sensing the world. Parents say no to their toddlers all the time, when all their child wants to do is sense the world around him. Pity, isn't it! Overdose on the senses is what I say, all the way through life."

I have no answer. So often I am too busy producing the moment for others, just like now, to pay attention to my senses. I rarely think about the experience and what I am feeling until it is over.

We make our way to the center, pushing aside thousands of little bugs that are scattered on top of the surface, and then stop, and drift. I lean my elbows on the seat behind me and stretch out, gazing up at the cloudless sky, and let the sun bring a glow to my face. The stifling buildup of habit would have kept me onshore had it not been for Joan, I find myself thinking. Her uncomplicated abandonment has helped me step out beyond my rut. I gaze over the side of the boat. We seem suspended inside a reflection. I've never experienced a pond quite this way. And then my bliss is jarred by a thought. What will my life be like when my husband returns? The very thought makes me anxious and my body tenses. It's been such an idyllic couple of months with Joan as my muse. My day suddenly goes sour with thoughts of the unknown future. I sit up and startle Joan. "You know we won't be able to do this when my husband returns."

"Really," she answers in a monotone voice. "Why not? I'm out here having a marvelous time, not thinking about Erik just now. Besides, he'd probably be applauding our little excursion if he knew about it." She leans over the side of the boat, cups her hand, and splashes me. The cool water hits me straight in the face and shocks me into laughter and out of my maudlin thoughts. I lean over and do the same. We are, for the moment, two silly girls without a care in the world—the brief minute or two of seriousness lost and gone for now.

"Where to now, captain?" I ask as the wind picks up and we begin to drift far off center.

"Let's see where the elements take us. That should be fun. It's a bit too soon to return to shore, wouldn't you say?"

I lie back once again, close my eyes, and allow my mind to go blank. The warm sun dries my wet jersey and damp face. Fifteen minutes or so must have elapsed when I next hear Joan's fragile soprano voice: "Row, row, row your boat, gently down the stream," she sings. She grabs the oars and pulls us away from the cove. "Merrily, merrily, merrily, merrily, life is but a dream. We were about to go amok," she shouts. "You take over," she says, gladly handing me the oars as she deftly swings her body around to face the bow, squinting in order to bring the far-off shore into focus. "I'm too delirious. Still, I'm afraid it's time to leave. We've just about gotten as much as we can out of this day, wouldn't you say?"

"You mean we've lived our dash," I quip.

"For now, I suppose."

I row slowly, thinking all the way back about how we had managed to stop our lives by simply floating about on a remote kettle pond.

"To leave my little cove was always sad," Joan says, thinking once again back to her childhood. "My time there had been stolen and secret. I might even have to fib or dodge questions when I got home, but no matter. The cove was mine and it would always be there for me."

"As is this pond," I say. "Thank you for this day and insisting that we overdose on our senses."

"There really isn't any other suitable way to be, is there, dear?"

I smile at her resolve. It occurs to me that I need to stop living on the surface or in the shallows, when drifting out over my head is always an option.

CHAPTER FIVE

WEAVING A LIFE

I feel as if my solitary year has flown by all too quickly, and I'm still filled with questions about my future. As the summer continues, my anxiety increases over my husband's inevitable return. I telephone Joan to quell my uneasiness.

"Joanie," I say somewhat frantically into the phone. "I was right. My husband is moving to the Cape, sometime in late September. He wants to leave the work world behind and experience his own year by the sea. I'd say I'm in a pickle, wouldn't you?"

"Not necessarily. Your fellow is simply ready to move on with his life. You can't fault him for that," she answers somewhat more jauntily than I had hoped. The way she calls him "my fellow" brings me up short; she makes it sound tender and possessive.

"What are you afraid of, dear?" she asks.

"That I'll turn back into a wife," I answer, "or the kind of wife I used to be."

"No you won't. You've tasted too much of the other. You'll see, it'll all happen slowly. You will have to give yourself time and space, but I'm certain he'll feel the same way."

"I'm not so sure. He is using the word 'we' an awful lot. I'm happy if he truly wants to come here and discover what is unlived in his own life, but I'm not so sure I'm ready to plunge back into the 'we' world." I pause and wait for a response. Doesn't she understand my predicament? Probably she has never wanted to hide from her husband. "Quite frankly, I'm not sure I ever want to live with another person," I blurt out, "let alone be married to one!"

"It seems to me that you'd best keep your focus on yourself. I'd continue to reach for the kind of dreams your year alone awakened in you before you start wondering whether you want to be married or not."

"Easy for you to say," I mumble.

"A long time ago, when I needed to get hold of my strengths and understand who I was becoming, I took to weaving. Although my husband had described the stages of life using little boxes and graphs, I always had trouble grasping their implications. Here I was married to the man who had mastered an explanation of identity and selfhood, and even he, or maybe especially he, couldn't help me figure it out. I had always thought of the self as a richly colored tapestry with each thread significant to the integrity of the whole. The more I struggled with my own crisis, the more I realized I had to make something. So I wove my life cycle on a loom. That might be something we could do together. What do you think?"

"I'm not sure I understand."

"You're having some sort of identity crisis, right? And your husband's return is putting all the more pressure on you to know who you are and where you stand. Correct?"

"Correct."

"Well, I detest preachy people, especially if they try to use their words to make them seem wise, and there is a great discrepancy in our ages, but I think my weaving project could help you," she says, sounding more than determined.

"How so?" I ask as I am becoming warily protective of what is left of my solitary independence, and her plan sounds time-consuming.

"Weaving your stages, dear, will help you finally see all the strengths you possess. It's important to know your strengths so you can lean on your truth, work with your struggles, and eventually become someone who sponsors herself. How's that for an explanation?"

"I'm impressed," I admit.

"Look. I'm guessing you've been expanding and developing for years but you simply haven't been able to digest it all. Doing something with your hands, rather than your head, is often the best route to clarity. When you weave your life together you will see how each stage has contributed to making the very unique woman you have turned out to be. Besides, we owe it to ourselves to always create something out of nothing. It's a weakness to just sit around and wait for a life to come to you. Am I making sense?"

"Sort of," I answer tentatively.

"How about it, then? I'd love to get my fingers moving along a loom once again, and it would be a fun project to share with you."

"Can I get back to you?" I stall.

"Certainly, dear. I'm not going anywhere."

And with that I hang up the receiver, knowing full well that my calendar is totally empty. Why am I hesitating? For one thing, I'm not particularly crafty; I haven't even managed to finish the scarf that I started knitting five years ago. And how am I really supposed to see my life in pieces of thread? But really, what else am I going to do with my spare time, wander around hoping for answers to appear out of the blue? At least weaving offers a focus. Besides, my talks with Joan up until now have done nothing but enhance and refresh my perspective. Refusing such a wise woman—one who has done a lion's share of pondering—would be almost as ridiculous as refusing piano lessons from Mozart! Ultimately, the chance to do something constructive wins out, and I call Joan back. "So, when do we start?"

"We're on? Oh, goody. I'll need a few days to gather supplies," she says, thinking aloud. "How about Thursday?"

"Sounds fine. Till then."

Five days later, on a most sultry summer afternoon, Joan arrives, singing. "Here comes the teacher . . . here comes the teacher." Her arms are laden with baskets and bags, and she has a huge bolt of fabric slung over her shoulder. "I haven't had a chance to weave in years," she bubbles once inside the door, looking puckishly beguiling. "I'm dying to get you on your way."

Without wasting a minute, she begins unpacking her wares—skeins of yarn in every conceivable color, darning needles, scissors, and cardboard. "I even wrote about this," she says, slapping a book down on the kitchen table. "If, as a last resort, after we actually get into the weaving and you can't make sense of it, you can always read my theory."

I reach for the yellow-jacketed book entitled *Wisdom and the Senses* and begin flipping through the pages. "But right now we're trying to stay out of our heads, dear, remember?" I watch her line up eight brilliantly colored bundles of yarn and explain that each color depicts the eight basic strengths—some I already have and some I will gain as I go along. "Things like purpose, competence, will, fidelity," she informs me matter-of-factly. "You'll soon see how great you are," she says, while reaching for a large piece of cardboard.

"Really," I say, not entirely convinced.

"Here," she continues, "we need to cut the cardboard into two large squares." She hands me the scissors so I can do the same. "What we are about to do is not about intellect; it's about touch. I want you to stop wondering who you are and actually begin to feel and touch your very essence. That's the point of weaving. As you work the threads, you'll gain an entirely new perspective."

I'm beginning to see a modicum of sense in Joan's quirky metaphors, having heard before that traditional cultures insist that their young learn the "how" of such crafts as papermaking or pottery, so they might understand the process of life, from origin to finality. Still, the questions keep coming.

"What's the cardboard for?" I ask.

"Our looms. We'll be making everything from scratch," she answers.

"But I pictured working on a real loom," I admit, not able to mask my disappointment in the makeshift apparatus that make me feel as though I'm back in kindergarten.

As if intuiting my confusion and impatience, Joan rushes to the kitchen table and begins to unravel the bolt of fabric she lugged in.

"How gorgeous," I exclaim, slightly dazzled.

"Well, I should think so," she says, "because this is my life, staring us in the face. See how the stripes are connected to one another. Each represents a different stage. As it turns out, I'm this well-knit human being, made from thousands of interlocking threads. Amazing, isn't it? The threads represent various events and experiences. What's more, I've come to know that each and every moment has colored who I am, who I'm becoming. Isn't that fun? But enough talk!" she says, interrupting herself and moving toward more comfortable chairs. "Let's get on with it."

I follow her example and punch holes in all four sides of my cardboard as she measures equal strands of gray yarn. "First, we need to make a warp," she explains.

"A what?"

"It's a way to create a framework for the tapestry, the consistent element of support . . . no different than our skeletons, which keep our bodies intact. The warp keeps the tapestry together," she says, absolutely full of herself.

"We'll begin by tying strands of gray from top to bottom, making sure that each strand is smooth and equally taut."

"Why are we using gray?"

"Gray represents the negative pulls and conflicting elements—those challenges put in our way that we're made to resolve. Because gray is a lifeless, somewhat dull shade, it reminds me to reach beyond the dull to the more colorful aspects of living."

"You certainly do that," I jest, but she barely reacts, intent now on creating her background. I follow her lead and work diligently, concentrating hard, even though my fingers are not nearly as nimble as hers. I'm only on my fourth strand when I notice she is way ahead of me. I swear under my breath from weary exasperation.

She must sense my frustration. "Take your time," she counsels. "There are no shortcuts to creating a tapestry or a life, for that matter...no speeding up the process. Besides, the pure monotony of it will give you the time and empty space to muse. There's a saying that suggests that those who work with their hands are laborers; those who work with their hands and heads are craftsmen; and those who work with their hands, heads, and hearts are artists. A woodcarver told me that. Isn't it a lovely sentiment? I think we're aiming to be artists today."

I feel suddenly humbled and force myself to slow

down. Eventually my shoulders drop as I develop a rhythm timed to the classical music on the radio. When did I last use my hands to create something solid and original? As a child I spent hours making potholders on a small metal loom. I wonder what ever became of them.

Joan is smoothing out the loose ends that extend across the entire bottom of her loom. "Fringe benefits," she murmurs, touching them lovingly. "We all come with fringe benefits . . . they're developed in utero. They have nothing to do with how you live. They come with you at birth and you've no choice but to work with them."

"You mean genes?" I ask.

"Something like that," she answers. "Really, they are the innate qualities that each of us arrives with . . . some of us are upbeat while others are melancholic, for instance. No one is born without attitudes and predilections of some sort or another. We're made to integrate them into our way of being as we go along. You can't get away from the fact that you came with a lot of stuff, and all those fringe benefits demand attention. Besides, it would be dumb to allow them to lie dormant," she insists, her enthusiasm pushing me onward.

"Well, I'm glad to know that I started out with something," I quip.

"Look, dear. A life, like a good weaving, is even. The struggle, the pull and tug are everything."

"Now that thought takes some digesting," I say, suggesting we stop for lunch. An hour or two later, after tuna fish sandwiches and several glasses of iced tea, I have finally finished my damn warp and I'm ready to add some color to my loom. "So we start with a light blue yarn," she says, and passes me a handful of equally cut pieces of yarn.

"Why light blue?" I ask while threading my needle.

"It just seems like the right color for infancy—watery, pale, and without much punch. Once you've tied on the yarn, make sure to keep each row taut. Energy is generated in the tension. And if you miss a stitch or double up on the thread," she continues with her instruction, "you'll notice the entire pattern changes. Interesting metaphor for life, isn't it?"

I certainly have dropped more than my share of stitches over a lifetime, I find myself thinking—when I just couldn't hold on, let others take control. It sure did change not only the way I look but also the way I look at things. There is method to her madness. I decide to listen more carefully.

"We'll only do a few pale blue rows," she says, "and then call it a day. Probably we should weave a stage a day—that way we will dig down deep into each period of our lives."

She's lost me again, but I'm intrigued enough to remain committed. "The strength we get in infancy is hope. Through your life hope continues to be the vital strength—the lifeline for growth and development. If a baby is held, swaddled, nursed, and sung to, the child will develop trust and hope. You seem to have lots of hope, dear. You must have been very loved as an infant," she says, looking up and eyeing me thoughtfully, waiting for my comment.

"Well, I was a wanted child, I know that for certain," I answer, "especially since I was a girl and my parents already had a boy. My arrival made us a perfect family of four. They even had me christened twice—once in New York City where my grandparents lived and then again in Buffalo, New York, where I was born."

"Lucky for you, dear. I wasn't so fortunate, being the third born to a mother who was miserable in the outback of Canada, away from the New York society she adored. She suffered a nervous breakdown soon after I came along, and my grandmother was called into service. As it turned out, that was the best thing that could have ever happened to me. My nama loved me—in fact she adored everything I did, even the trouble I got into. She was always applauding my actions and ideas. It only takes one, you know, one person to utterly approve of you and you're on the way. But we're getting ahead of ourselves. Nama's influence came to me during early childhood and the play age."

I am beginning to see the relationship between weaving and my life, so I pick up some more yarn to do a few more rows to represent the fullness of my beginning before moving on to the second stage. Already forgetting her resolve to weave just one stage a day, she hands me the ball of orange yarn to begin measuring and cutting.

"Orange is for the toddler time . . . when you begin to develop autonomy. The strength earned is a strong will," she explains. "Toddlers require much praise and applause as they strive to eat, walk, and explore on their own."

My thoughts go immediately to Mamie, a wonderful woman who lived in our duplex when I was two or three and who absolutely adored me. "There was this woman with no children who doted on me," I say. "Especially since my mother was hell-bent on doing everything by the book. Mamie, in contrast, would insist we make magic together. Her house had secret closets and cupboards full of candy and she always wanted to play. One day we scoured the kitchen floor for no other reason than to let popcorn pop out of the kettle and onto the floor, where we sat waiting to scoop it up with our hands and eat it."

"Good for her. Was she in your life for a long time?" Joan asks.

"Not long enough. We moved when I was about seven. It was heart-wrenching. I don't suppose I really ever got over it. From there on in, I became chubby and somewhat sad—at least that's what my childhood snapshots tell me. Life felt lonely. Something very significant was gone. She was my major source of approval and suddenly there was less applause for my accomplishments."

"It happened to me when I was sent to boarding school," Joan admits, "away from Nama and anything familiar. What was worse, I was the youngest child there and never really fitted in. But then I found a teacher who was a bright light. Her name was Miss Luke. She was a wonderful storyteller. Her dedication to the classics and great literature involved me so. Whatever the reason, I was ready for what she had to offer, and I absorbed her every thought. My reaction to her acted as a sort of challenge to both of us," she says, her voice trailing off as if she were far away. "People can be a great source of strength for each other, don't you think?"

I nod.

"It wasn't Miss Luke who inspired me necessarily," she continues, "but what I saw in her and the way I reacted to her that made all the difference." She sits back and closes her eyes briefly, as if to cement the memory of that time, and then, a few moments later, she comes alive again. "Always remember that strength comes from adversity," she quietly insists, while cutting strands of the green yarn that will represent the play stage. "I can't say it enough. We grow from those emotional conflicts. Our fate can be altered for the better if only we have the courage to embrace the opposites. That's the paradox. Everyone wants to walk under a rainbow, but it's the negative pulls that force us to reach a little further, do a bit more, make the extra effort. That's why the toddler, as he seeks conflict and tests the limits, is developing character."

"So all my mistakes haven't been in vain, after all!" I joke. "I had a hard time obeying the rules."

"Me too!" she all but exclaims with glee. "You were probably scolded as much as I when you were little. Most children are, when they disobey and do naughty things. But going ahead and doing them anyway probably made you plenty willful. That's what I like about you—your daring to be different and your initiative. I think you got a lot of strength out of your childhood, despite the good intentions of your parents. And, I'm guessing that you insisted on staying a bit longer than normal in the play stage."

"Oh yeah? How can you tell?"

"Your compassion. You must have playacted a lot as a

child, developing an empathy for the other's lot in life. That's what happens when you pretend. You're made to look at the other person's lot in life, so that today, you have a tenderness for unappreciated people."

I'm speechless. Especially because I view myself as being selfish, at least this year, having run away from everyone and everything.

As we stitched we shifted topics of conversation like dancers shift their bodies to accommodate the music. Our fingers pushed through rows of orange, green, yellow, and dark blue yarn, and I began to pull the tenets of my life together, gaining strength and self-knowledge every stitch of the way. My childhood was beginning to reappear on my loom with all its accompanying craziness and drama. What was most fascinating is that I could see how I had formed the very core of me. I was the origin of my own values. As I connected the stories and stages of my life I began to feel that I truly had a self—one that could no longer be taken from me.

"I think I'm getting it," I tell my teacher after our fourth session. And just to ensure that I don't regress, I've taken to carrying a few strands of braided yarn in my pocket, frequently fingering the colors to remind me of the generous amounts of hope, will, purpose, and competence that are mine for the keeping. What's more, because we managed to get through adolescence and beyond and I'm bursting with self-knowledge, I suspect I am more than prepared to begin a marriage again—at least more prepared than the first time around.

There is method to her madness, I think. At the very least she has gotten me to sit and pay attention to my past and present. Then I was made to create a product with my hands. Interwoven in these two activities was a chance to listen to her whimsy as well as her wisdom. I stare at my strengths as symbolized on my little loom. It's time, not only to embrace myself, but join the human race once again.

CHAPTER SIX

DANCE BEYOND
THE BREAKERS

Summer has passed far too quickly and Robin is planning to arrive quite soon after Labor Day. With his formal life behind him, he says that he is eager to explore the unknown—live without constriction. When I fell silent about his plans during a recent phone conversation, I felt him shrivel.

I could get excited about his newfound fervor if I didn't know that the man I have been married to for so long tends to be a homebody and is somewhat lazy in his leisure moments. Besides that, the word *retirement* has me extremely anxious. The work world provided a form to which he was made to adhere. I, in turn, have had free reign over my day, knowing I had no obligations around him until evening.

I worry that while I want to take off in new directions, he will simply want to sit by the fire. And how will he feel about my relationship with Joan? Although we've had conversations about her, I'm not sure that he realizes just how much we are a part of each other's lives.

But although Joan stresses the importance of holding on to a sense of self, she has also cautioned me not to set self and relationship too strictly against each other. "You could stand to melt a little, dear," she suggested. I'm not entirely sure what she means, but I am certainly hopeful that the woman I've become still has room for the man in her life.

Such is my state of mind on the day of Robin's arrival as I drive to The Squire, a local watering hole to which I have invited a variety of people to celebrate his future. I've dubbed the event a "change of life" party, hoping the theme will add humor to the occasion. Although he basically detests large gatherings, I felt that a party would soften the awkwardness we were sure to feel after having been apart for so long. Besides, I want him to meet some of the people I've come to know and admire—fishermen, artists, and tradesmen, those folks who make up the Cape's off-season population. Of course, I've invited Joan Erikson as well.

As I park the car and approach the restaurant, it feels reminiscent of all those years I had dinner waiting when he came home from the office, or the Friday summer afternoons when I would leave the beach at two o'clock to prepare for his weekend visit. I've enjoyed my vacation from marriage, and as I draw nearer the restaurant my anxiety intensifies. But once inside the door of this dark and cozy seaside pub, I spot several friends waiting for something to happen and I am able to push my uncertainty aside.

"Is he really on his last drive up from New York?" one of my friends asks.

"Yep, it's his final commute. Today ends his career in education as far as I know. Let's get a glass of wine."

As we make our way over to the bar, several more friends ramble in and soon there is an eager din. But why not? Hardly anyone on the Cape ever gets out midweek, and it doesn't hurt the spirit any that I'm paying the bar bill. In addition, we're in one funky setting, complete with a wooden carving of a sailor and his woman, she with a delicious smile, he tweaking her nipple. The thirty balloons sent by a friend have ascended to all parts of the ceiling, and the bartender has put on some very lively music.

Just as people are beginning to wonder if there is a husband after all, the man of the hour appears, a little road weary but clearly exhilarated. I move to embrace him, aware that all eyes are watching our reaction to each other. He holds me tight. "Hi, baby . . . it's good to be home," he whispers. "It's been a long time coming."

His sentiment both warms and startles me. I've not truly come to grips with this shared path. Still, I've come to know that this is my place and he is indicating that it is his as well. I pull away, embarrassed that our private moment is public, and lead him to the nearest guest to begin the introductions.

In minutes he is surrounded by well-wishers and I step away from his side to watch him handle the moment like a politician at a fund-raiser, a distinct difference from the man I used to know who had a hard time masking his distaste for most social interaction. Soon he heads for the bar and settles onto a stool next to Joan Erikson, who is happily sipping a glass of port.

"You must be Joan," I overhear him say. "I've heard a lot about you."

"That I'm naughty and nice?" she quips, immediately diffusing any formality before it has a chance to develop.

"According to my wife you are an original, eager to deviate from the path. I hear you have a great capacity for play. It's time I did more of that."

"That's easy to do here," she says, and then, as if she feels it important to mark this transition of his, she changes the subject and asks him what he will miss most about his former life.

"The students," he answers. "That's where all the meaning is."

I can barely hear what follows—something about the

rewards of teaching, watching youth develop, celebrating their successes. I'm suddenly feeling very good about throwing this party.

"Shouldn't there be a toast or something?" someone whispers in my ear.

Joan had urged me to get a gift. "A little ceremony never hurt any party or transition," she had argued. So I climb onto the seat of my bar stool and clink my glass to get everyone's attention. "To my husband," I shout, above the music and the crowd, "and all that is unfinished about him. Instead of the expected gold watch, honey, I'm offering you a tide clock—gone forever is linear time. You'll soon give yourself over to the rhythms of the sea."

The applause drowns out the music and becomes even louder when a virtual stranger approaches Robin with a pair of scissors in his hand. "You'll not be needing this anymore," he shouts and cuts off Robin's necktie and then tosses it to the rafters.

"Why thank you, sir," my husband replies, a bit shocked, but laughing heartily nonetheless, and then returns his attention to Joan.

"What do you do out here?" I hear him ask Joan. "Or, more specifically, what do you do all winter long?"

"Whatever you like," she says boldly. "That's the beauty of this life. You leave all the rigid rules behind."

"Sounds good to me," he says, but I wonder if he really means it. Breaking rules entails risk and rebellion, two ideals he has always shied away from. Perhaps that's all about to change? I hope so.

Eventually the crowd thins out and we are left alone— Robin and me, and Joan, who is waiting for a taxi to take her home. "I'm going to have another drink," my husband announces, hopping off his bar stool. Joan hands him her glass. "I'll have another, too," she says, and then winks at me as if to say things are going well. When he returns and suggests we order some food, we move to a more comfortable booth and settle in. Joan adjusts her purple velvet shawl in such a way that it frames her face and makes her look positively radiant in the flickering candlelight. I suddenly feel old and dowdy in comparison.

"Look at those folks dancing over there in the corner," Joan says as we turn to crane our necks. "Dance is so absolutely glorious. There's no end to what you can do with pure energy."

Robin nods in agreement, and then surprises me by continuing. "It was one of the first ways I found to express myself when I was a kid. Being tall, skinny, and awkward, I could barely control my limbs. Then one day I heard the Big Bopper on the radio."

"The who?" Joan interrupts.

"He was one of the early rock-and-roll singers. You know, 'Chantilly Lace with a pretty face,'" he almost sings the lyrics. "Suddenly, I couldn't contain myself. When that music came on, I was out of my seat making all kinds of contortions."

"And feeling flexible, too," Joan insists.

"Well, I wasn't exactly smooth or suave, but I felt good—a connection to something big and powerful. For the first time my body was in a groove."

"I think when I danced for the first time, I was enthralled with myself as well," she says, her thoughts drifting off to another time. "I remember saying to myself, I can do this, I can very obviously do this! It's a wonderful thing to make use of every bit of your body," she says, in between sips of port, "especially with modern dance, which isn't restricting. Rather, it's about breaking boundaries. Right now, though," she says, suddenly sounding sad, "I'm challenged by this damn body. It doesn't always do what I want it to."

"Well, let's see how well it can move on the dance floor," Robin says spontaneously, and rising quickly, he helps her out of the booth before she has a chance to refuse. I watch as he leads her away, this tall middle-aged man about to waltz with a ninety-something woman to an

Elton John hit, no less. *"It's a little bit funny, this feeling inside, I'm not one of those who can easily hide. . . ."*

I listen to the lyrics, watch my husband, and shake my head. After all those introverted years when I would poke and prod him to be gallant at a party, dance with the hostess, seek out the wallflowers, here he is jumping right in with an elderly woman. Some of the other patrons have stopped eating to watch, but Joan doesn't notice. She's caught up in the moment, her eyes transfixed on Robin as he begins to twirl her around, once and then twice. She's not the least bit embarrassed by the nature of exhibition, as I would be, always hiding my private madness.

He holds her close to him for a moment as if he is afraid she might wilt from the motion. But her body is cooperating, and she keeps going, dancing off now on her own, raising her arms toward the ceiling, swaying her hips to the rhythm, and grinning from ear to ear.

When the music ends, several patrons applaud the spectacle they've created. No one but Robin wants it to end, and he leads her back to the booth and sinks into the seat, his face flushed and forehead damp.

"Wow, what a moment!" Joan exclaims, happily collapsing next to me. "So much good energy goes into a dance! Couldn't you just feel it?"

"Looks like you guys could have danced right out the door," I say, delighted in her delight.

"And down the street and onto the beach. Why not?" she laughs. "Dance beyond the breakers, that's what I say . . . be willing to go as far as you dare. Hell, it's one of the few legitimate ways to be sexy and sensuous," she says, her naughty twinkle appearing again. "The motion of the whole thing . . . and the flexibility it evokes! The lucky ones are those that grow up near water where everything is in motion—you crave it the rest of your life," she says, reaching for my water glass and taking a gulp.

"I grew up on a river," Robin says. "The Shrewsbury. I used to go fishing on its banks as a little boy and watch it drift by. Do you really think that's why someone likes to move?"

"I sure do. It's a force that gets into your blood and stays there."

"You should have seen him in Africa!" I interject. "He would get going at tribal gatherings, grooving to the beat of the drums and their minor tin instruments, and soon be enveloped in the fold."

"I'm not surprised," Joan answers, smiling as she visualizes him bopping around. "Dancing has been my salve for years. Primitives know the power of dance. That's how they call on their spirits. I'm always assuming that everyone else in the world knows what good medicine it is."

And then, without missing a beat, she raises her glass: "'Dance when you're broken open,'" she says dramatically, reciting a line from another poem she has committed to memory, "and, 'Dance if you've torn the bandage off, Dance in the middle of the fighting, Dance in your blood, Dance, when you're perfectly free.' Anyway, that's how I feel about it," she concludes, taking a final gulp of port.

I glance over at Robin, who is dumbfounded. Surely we are having the same thought. How could anyone so old be so alive?

"I want to be as loose as you guys," I say, "but I never could follow Robin's outrageous moves. Mostly, I'd end up sitting out the next dance, hoping he'd find a better partner."

"There should never be any set way to dance. It's about losing yourself and giving your body over to the music," Joan replies soothingly.

"Yeah, well, I've hardly graduated from my dancing school years where we were taught only the waltz or the fox-trot," I complain.

"I was taught the same or worse, but then I was driven to develop my own motion. I won't let you get away with that excuse," she says. "You've got to start playing some of that Big Bopper music around your cottage," she continues, looking at Robin, "and get this girl going with the flow. She's turned wild and salty, that's for sure, but I'm still trying to unravel her here and there."

Unbeknownst to me, Robin has ordered from the raw bar, and we dive into a huge platter of oysters and little-necks. Moments later, the bartender sends over a bottle of champagne, compliments of the house. "Always remember, my dears," Joan says by way of a toast, "that no matter how hard you dance, not everyone will clap." She lifts her glass to both of us. "At the very least, from here on in, you'll be creating your own rules. Take your dreams by the hand and let them float. It's a gift being your own person. In any case, it's pretty deadly not to be. You two have your lives to get in order. I'm sure I'll be seeing you again soon." And with that, she gulps down the bubbles, rises from her seat, and is off.

I follow her as she makes her way nimbly toward the door and then turn my gaze back to Robin. He has leaned back into the booth, stretching his long legs so that his feet now rest on the seat across from his. The man is mellow—seemingly content to be precisely where he is. I feel my previous concerns about us slip away. Joan had told me that certain aspects of relationships shed their skin and then show up again in a different texture, form, or color. *"It's a little bit funny, this feeling inside..."* sings Elton. How nice to welcome back feelings, warm feelings, that is, toward my husband. It feels like the beginning again. By being open, welcoming, and ready to receive, grace happens. Always be willing to dance. That's Joan's motto. No more wallflower for me.

"Well, this has certainly been an interesting first night," Robin says, interrupting my thoughts and taking another sip of champagne. "You, me, an old lady, and a bar."

"A hint of more good things to come," I say.

CHAPTER SEVEN

LOVE KNOTS

W here are you off to?" Robin asks as I stuff papers and notebooks into my briefcase, preparing to venture out on this cold and windy January day.

"My office," I answer abruptly, already half an hour behind the schedule I set in my New Year's resolution—writing five days a week from eight to one.

"I didn't know you had one," he says, puzzled now and more than curious. "Did you rent a place?"

"No, silly," I answer, while I hastily run a brush through my hair and apply lipstick. "I told you that Joan Erikson offered me a room in her house."

"But you seemed quite content with the space you created on the porch. Why can't you work there?"

"That was before I was attempting to write about my year alone. It's impossible to do that now that you've returned. Your very presence keeps jarring me into daily reality when I'm trying to reflect back."

He looks forlorn in a way that used to keep me by his side, but not today. I grab my parka, scarf, and car keys. "Do you have any plans?" I ask, attempting to show a mild interest in his day.

"Well, there's no golf in this weather. I'm not sure what I'll do."

"See you at dinner then," I say, and head out, congratulating myself for protecting my valued time. Joan and I have found some time to ourselves on days when Robin plays golf. Other than that, she has joined us for the occasional dinner and I have continued to take her to church and special events. But those precious days when we would let serendipity guide our way have all but disappeared. Reawakening a marriage takes more time than I thought.

The drive to Joan's takes no more than five minutes. I'm eager for the solitude her house will provide and for the personal revelations that were coming so frequently during our weaving sessions. Our plan is that both of us will write separately in the morning and then come together to weave in the afternoon. The last session, some two months ago, kept me hanging, and I've been ruminating over my lost youth ever since. We had been discussing the fifth stage, which is about finding one's own personal identity and being true to the self. Joan offered many examples of how she worked to become her own person. The more tales she offered, the more I realized how I had shrunk from the task altogether. In fact, I had basically avoided the fifth stage in order to feed my insatiable appetite for intimacy and love, both of which are meant to come in the sixth stage. Now it feels like I'm doing it again—giving more time to relationship and less time to myself. Will I ever learn to take my own life more seriously?

It is in this mood and with these questions that I arrive at her house, let myself in the back door with the extra key she had made for me, climb the stairs to my office, and sink into an old wooden swivel chair. How nice to be in my own little space surrounded by a few precious belongings. I've brought several rocks from the beach for paperweights, a shell mobile that dangles from the ceiling above my desk, and there are several wooden In and Out boxes to store the unfinished and finished work. A tidy office is such a shelter, buttressing me on all sides, and just now giving me a cozy sense of security. I empty my book bag of loose papers and colored pens, turn on some music, and mercifully lose myself in the writings of Wallace Stegner, as his work usually stimulates a thought in me that eventually gets me to put pen to paper. Several hours pass before I hear the back door open.

"Hello," I call down the stairs. "Is it you?"

"It is I," she says, almost singing her response. "Are you ready for me? I brought us a sandwich from the deli—a vegetarian roll-up. It is oozing with good things. Shall I put the kettle on?"

"I'll be right down" I say, eager for diversion. She plants a kiss on each cheek and then goes back to arranging the sandwich plates while I prepare the tea.

"How's Erik?" I ask, assuming she has been at the nursing home.

"He's fine, dear. Thanks for asking. We had a pleasant morning. I bundled him up and we went for a walk around the grounds. The trouble with institutions is that you can't ever see the seasons change. One day just seems like another if you are inside all the time."

I am once again amazed, listening to her chatter as if her husband were still able to share in anything they used to do together. She is still getting optimum pleasure out of this relationship that has changed so. Her attitude encourages me to keep my whining at bay.

As the teapot whistles, I pour two cups of ginger tea, set them on a tray with honey and sugar cubes, and head for the living room, with Joan following closely behind. She isn't in her chair more than a second when I notice her eyeing the basket of yarn.

"Are you up for weaving today? It's Thursday, you know."

"That would be great. I've missed our sessions. It seems years ago that we sat blissful, musing over our pasts."

"I've been trying to remain scarce for the past few months while at the same time dying to know what you're up to. We haven't really had that much time alone, have we, dear? But I do know that a man needs to feel he's got his wife right there. I figured that's what was going on."

"Sorry for my absence. As much as I promised not to turn back into a wife, I've felt the need to be available and helpful. It seems that change affects men far more than it affects women."

"Poor souls. Their identity is so wrapped up in their careers. Without that, they're lost. Men demand such peculiar things of themselves. They think it is a necessity to be a particular way instead of just being themselves."

"No kidding. But finally I realized that there is really nothing I can do about helping him reinvent his life. Weaving taught me that. We each need to look at and take hold of our own strengths. Perhaps you could pass a little Eriksonian actuality on to Robin."

"That might be fun. I do think he's absolutely smashing, you know."

"Oh, you're just saying that because he asked you to dance."

"Well, that could be part of it, but really, I'm serious . . . he's quite something."

"How so?"

"I like how he gets involved in our conversations. He is right there and quite eager to know new things."

"Hmmmm. Come to think of it, around you he is always spontaneous."

"Maybe he actually does know what he's come to. In any case, I think you've got a keeper."

I find myself hoping that she is right.

"But there's more going on. What am I missing? What's the faraway look I see in your face?"

"I suppose I'm troubled about love. I'm not feeling it. Oh, we are getting along all right, but so far we seem like roommates, not husband and wife."

"It's all about pacing, dear. You've both been hibernating—can't expect to crawl out of your caves without allowing for a little time to wake up, adjust to the light, get some food in your stomachs."

"It's more than that. I've been haunted by my weaving—staring at it hanging over my desk—realizing that there is a big hole in the fifth stage. I never bothered to really develop myself—skipped right over me in order to get to love. What's worse, I seem to be repeating myself again, today, as we reignite the marriage. It's frightening." My thoughts continue to tumble out one after another in confused succession until I grab hold of my loom and begin plucking at the rainbow of woven colors like a tennis player checking the strings on her racket.

"But don't you see," she says finally as she reaches into the basket for the red yarn and quickly snips us some strands, "that's what your year alone was all about, dear. You instinctively knew you needed time to get back to that raw material person—your words, not mine—and you've done a damn good job of it. You did back up and revisit the fifth stage. There's a whole new person in this relationship—you!"

"I'm not sure my husband sees it that way. He's moved back in and it appears that he sees our future life together as business as usual. Getting him to view our life differently is not going to be easy. You can see from how I've cut down on our visits that I'm slipping back into those old familiar patterns."

"Behaving like you did before is inevitable," she says, sounding momentarily discouraging, which shocks me. "But be prudent in your calling this time around. Pick and choose what you enjoy doing around the home and what can best be left to him. After all, he has been functioning on his own for a year. I'm sure he's become very capable, if not willing to participate on new terms," she says to buoy my confidence.

"I hope so," I answer warily.

I can see her searching for a personal anecdote to prove her point. "When I was into writing a lot of poetry and prose," she starts, "I bought a typewriter. Erik caught on rather quickly that I could be of some service to him. He gave me a letter to type quite soon thereafter, and I was pleased to oblige. But the following day he left me three or four letters. After a week of this, I simply gave the type-writer away. It's not a big thing, I'm telling you, but the point is that he came to respect my role in my own life as much I respected his."

I find her tale curiously nourishing, having always been one to confuse serving with loving. I brush away a tear, hoping she doesn't notice my reddened cheeks. How did I ever get such a warped sense of loving—not under-standing the reciprocal nature of it? "I really did think it was all about pleasing the man and making him happy," I admit.

"Many a woman makes it a goal to know her man without knowing herself, first. She sees loving him as the solution to her problems, but love soon becomes the center of her problem. She is thinking rather than feeling her way through the relationship and eventually becomes isolated from the very essence of herself. That is a tragedy," she explains.

"Nonetheless, that's what I did. If he was happy, I was happy, simply because I had made him happy."

"Love was coming to you—you weren't going toward it. You were just avoiding trouble and thinking that was a reward. What a pity. There wasn't enough strength in it," she surmises.

"Funny you should be telling me this," I say. "A therapist once told me that good deeds do not always equal something in return."

"Well, in any case, I always envisioned marriage as a collaboration," she continues. "Mutuality, reciprocity, interdependence are the keys to the game. If you don't have them, what's the point?"

"Hmmm," I answer, "but not easily accomplished if you didn't start out that way. How did you arrive at that concept, after all?"

"I want to credit Erik, but actually it came from both of us. We were each driven to find our individual identities. Perhaps it was our childhoods—he was agonized over not knowing his birth father, and I felt little or no affirmation from my troubled mother. We must have sensed a deep need to know ourselves better if we were ever to know anyone else. It certainly wasn't intentional, but now as I try to explain it, I think it makes sense."

"It sure does," I answer, feeling envious of her pure luck, or karma, and suddenly feeling very sad that my self-hood is only just beginning to take hold.

"Look, dear," she says, eyeing me thoughtfully, "we all start out mushy and dewy-eyed. That's puppy love. Inevitably those feelings turn into functional love—when you have time for little else but tending to children and holding on to jobs. The only way to reignite a relationship is for each partner to separate, either literally or figuratively, in order to return to themselves, to develop long-forgotten talents or dreams, and most importantly, to learn to accept their own underpinnings. We're all loaded up with them. Turn your loom over and you'll see what I mean."

The other side is hideous—a mess of knots, uneven stripes, and loose ends.

"The underpinnings show us where we got off the

track," she explains, matter-of-factly. "I look at all the knots I've tied and say to myself, this knot in early childhood got me into that knot in adolescence, and wow, look at how uneven the rows became until I worked through that problem or straightened out that course."

"Okay. Okay. I get your point," I answer impatiently, tired now of yet another metaphorical explanation. "But I would just as soon avoid my underpinnings and keep my eyes focused on the pretty side. That's my husband's attitude as well."

"Most people have that attitude. But then you've stopped the process. Eventually, you'll simply congeal. When you are willing to pull back and look at your neglected dreams and foibles, you bring a newfound energy into your partnership. You learn to respect what makes you an individual and you learn to accept the other person's quirks as well. It isn't easy work. The big trap most of us fall into is believing that love and joy always go together. It can't possibly be so because truth comes with love and many times truth is not so playful because of its honesty."

My needle is now going up and under, up and under, at a speed like never before, and the red yarn is splashing across my weaving in broader strokes than I had originally intended. I'm intrigued by Joan's thoughts about adult love, but I'm also anxious simply to move on to some other stage over which I'll have more control.

"What's your hurry?" she asks, noticing my haste. "Don't rush the process, especially if you haven't resolved your feelings around it. And while you weave, ask yourself, where is the strength in your union? You came with stuff and he came with stuff. What's worth encouraging in your togetherness?"

"What about passion?" I ask, realizing we had all but avoided the subject. "Do we ever get that back?" I lean back and take a sip of my lukewarm tea awaiting her answer.

"Oh, it can't be fabricated," she finally utters. "Passion is a force, a direction you are moved to. It comes when you are open and vulnerable. Didn't we feel it at Robin's party—you and he, he and I—palpable energy between us all. And it happened because we were open to it. Still, passion is only a lofty word if you stay closed and not open. All the words attached to the stages are so grand. Only when we turn them into verbs and connect them with action do they make sense. Always remember, dear, that theory without action has no strength at all."

"Of course," I murmur, picking up my loom once again.

As I work the red yarn through the gray field I am humbled, feeling the emotion of the process as well as her love for me.

"You get love by participating in it," she says, sensing now that I'm finally grasping this stage. "That goes for all the other strengths too."

And so during the cold winter months I found warmth in her continuing messages and affirmations while watching the growth of my ever-changing tapestry, which remains unfinished because I am unfinished as well. "Leave room for the rest of your life," Joan cautions. "You've got lots left to accomplish. Generativity, the strength of stage seven, goes on until you depart."

There is no lost future. The life I might have lived is beginning to take hold. Ever so slightly I am moved from resignation to a sense of possibility.

CHAPTER EIGHT

MIGHT AS WELL MAKE
THE MOST OF IT

I t is a strange spring afternoon—dull air, brooding skies, weather that does not invigorate. I've been calling Joan all day, leaving messages on her machine. "What's on your mind?" her recorded voice asks the caller. Usually I say something trite and she always gets right back to me. But not today. I make one last try and find her clever message more than frustrating. "You're on my mind. Where are you?" I shout, and then I plunk down the receiver, realizing suddenly that something must be very wrong. I grab the car keys and take off, not bothering to stop at her house. There are only two places she could be: the beach or the nursing home. Instinct tells me she is at the latter.

Once inside and past the front desk, I start down a corridor that seems darker than usual. The place feels like a morgue—no patients walking the halls, no wheelchairs or nurses with medicine carts, not even the usual piped-in music. A few steps later I am at the last door on the hall, an end room Joan requested to ensure privacy and remove them from the institutional atmosphere. I gently knock.

"Come in," her voice responds softly.

I nudge open the door and find her sitting upright with a phone book in her hand, her eyes telling me that something grave is occurring.

"Oh, it's you," she says, sounding relieved. "What a coincidence! I was just trying to find your phone number. Sit down, dear," she says, motioning to a nearby chair. "Erik's dying."

"What?" I gasp, sitting down beside her and quickly scanning the room for clues as to what is transpiring. I had thought it odd when I ran into her minister in the parking lot, who greeted me warmly. "I have another family to pay a call on," he had said. "You'll be a comfort to her, I'm sure." Only now do I understand the full implications of his comment.

I'm a confusion of feelings, feeling momentarily lost, unable to come up with consoling words, so I simply take her hand in mine. Her serene demeanor forces me to pull myself together. "What happened?" I ask. "You didn't mention that he was ill when we last spoke. Did he have a stroke?"

"An infection," she answers, shrugging her shoulders as if she has no idea how he could have contracted one.

"Can't something be done?"

Her eyes flash up, swimming with sudden tears. "Once before he was very ill and I brought him back. This time there are to be no heroics," she says with uncomplicated confidence, at peace, it seems, with his mortality. It's too much—love and grief in one place. I'm overwhelmed. Never having been at a deathbed before, I'm struck by the isolation of grief. It's an emotion that really can't be shared; it is hers to face and process. I can only offer solace when I sense her weariness taking over. What's more, there is no precedent for such a scene, no time for rehearsal. Not everyone can respond to the moment, which, fortunately, she does so well.

"Memories are like pearls," she says, filling the vacant space with a thought I can take hold of as she fingers a strand around her neck. "They make up a life," she continues. "You wear them and finger them and recall all you have and have been a part of."

"Yes," I agree halfheartedly, not certain where she is taking this.

"It's been quite a ride with Erik. So many grand times, mixed in with some harsh moments," she continues, her face looking pained while I try to remember some of her sad stories. "The best moments were the most simple . . . climbing to the top of a hillside surrounding Vienna, in the beginning of our courtship, me clad in a huge blue cape, he shivering in just a sweater. There was no alternative but to wrap us up in my cape." Her eyes are fiery now, a rush of color coming to her cheeks as she seems able to taste the very event. "Decorum went out the window." She laughs at herself. "We gave in to the moment, then and forever."

Her manner of receiving that which is presented will always be with her, I think. It is so like Joan to imbue this event with as much love and positive energy as all the others of her life. And what a pity for those of us who turn away from such a moment because it isn't what we planned, or because we simply can't handle it. Not Joanie! This moment was every bit as important as any other one she shared with Erik. She knew she needed, indeed wanted, to be utterly present until the end. My eyes drift over her shoulder to a dresser covered with framed pictures of happier times and events and beyond that to the bookshelf where she has carefully lined up volumes of Erik's work.

"I feel as though we should light some candles," Joan whispers in an uncertain tone.

"Would you like me to go look for some?" I ask, eager to have something to do.

"No, dear, that's all right. That would mean you'd have to leave me. We'll be fine without them."

I nod and turn from her, gazing out the uncurtained window and hear the rush hour—cars honking, brakes screeching, people involved in their everyday lives, hurrying to work and then back home again, passing this place without the slightest clue about the huge event taking place inside. I shake my head as I realize that dying is such a private act, momentous to be sure, but only to those very few involved.

Just then a frizzy-haired nurse pushes the door open with her hip and backs into the room carrying two trays. "You two must be famished," she says, placing the trays on the arms of our chairs. "I've brought you dinner. Salmon and peas. It looks good," she says, encouraging us to dig in—a strange thing to be doing beside the bed of a dying man.

"It does look delicious, dear," Joan says as she shovels a forkful of mashed potatoes into her mouth. "You will stay for dinner, won't you?"

"Of course. When last did you eat?" I ask her.

"This morning, I suppose. I'm famished. They have a great cook here," she continues, relishing the salmon dripping in hollandaise sauce.

"The scones that I brought to our weaving sessions were from here as well," she adds, and I can sense that she wants normal conversation for a while. "They've been sending me home with food ever since Erik moved in. Such a homey gesture, don't you think? The only thing they don't provide is port," she says, eyeing me now as if she hopes I might have a bottle stashed away somewhere.

"I could certainly oblige and go buy some, but I bet they keep some right here in the kitchen."

"Do you think?" she wonders, eager as a child.

"For medicinal purposes, of course." I wink. Just then a night nurse pops her head in the doorway. "Just checking," she says. "Everything all right?"

What an insensitive question, I think. How could anything possibly be all right in these circumstances? "It would be made better if we had some wine," I reply.

"Oh, that's not a problem at all," she utters. "Two glasses?"

Joan and I nod and then turn to each other, laughing over our momentary good fortune. "It is good to have you here, dear," she says warmly. "This is a first for me. I'm surprised that I've gone on so long and never had to face such a thing."

"That makes two of us," I say. "It's an honor, really. I'm just so glad I was around."

With dinner finished and wine consumed, it almost seems that we should pay the tab and leave. But alas, we've just had a brief respite from death and need to turn back to the task at hand. She moves toward the sink to dampen a washcloth and place it on her husband's feverish forehead. "There, there," she says, smoothing his white hair and whispering into his ear.

I feel uncomfortable, as though I should remove myself from this intimate scene. But each time I make my way to the door—once to go to the ladies' room, another to telephone my husband—she beckons for me to return. I nestle into the chair and lean my head back, sensing that it's going to be a long night. Why does this scene feel so familiar? I wonder. Ah, yes, I remember now. It reminds me of when I was giving birth. Labor had commenced, the pain was progressing, but then there was the wait—one of those few times I was ever made to surrender and relinquish all control. Interesting to find birth and death in the same category.

"Would you like to spend the night, Mrs. Erikson?" another nurse asks, as she comes into the room to remove our trays.

"I should think so," Joan answers with determination. "There isn't much happening back at my house."

"Can we make up a bed for you?"

"That won't be necessary," she says, firmly but politely.

"This *is* where I want to be. I do need a few things from the house, however. Dear," she turns to me, "do you suppose we could dash over there?"

Relieved to be spared, if only for a short time, from the enormous tension that has been building within me, I jump at the opportunity to get out into the night and the fresh air. A gentle mist is falling as we stumble toward the car, the porch lamp barely lighting the way, and off we go. I turn on the windshield wipers, and their gentle swishing all but eradicates our heavy thoughts for a time. Once inside her little house, we gather her things. Joan is in such a hurry that all I can see her do is stuff her medications and one or two other articles into a toiletries kit and we are ready to head back.

"I'm glad Erik didn't live with me in this house," she says, in one of the rare times she looks beyond the present moment. "That way it won't be so hard to return." I hug her fiercely before turning out the lights and heading back. We drive in silence, slowly, as I am not eager to begin the vigil once again. But alas, there is no way to lengthen a three-minute trip. We are back at the nursing home in no time.

"Oh, Joanie," I say as I watch her unpack her things, "you forgot to pack your nightgown."

"Oh no I didn't, dear," she says with a naughty twinkle.

She reaches for her leather toiletries kit, unzips it, and looking very much like a magician about to make a scarf appear from a top hat, she pulls out an aqua satin nightgown. "Might as well make the most of it," she says, stepping out of her jersey skirt and top to slip her nightgown over her head.

"I'll be down in the parlor, if you need me," I say, easing the door open and then closing it gently behind, leaning my head against the door. She's going to have this final night just the way she wants it, and so she should. The shrouded quiet of the place, which all but forbids noise, overcomes me and I suddenly feel a chilling loneliness for her as well as myself. Then, as if she intuited my longing, I hear not words, but song . . . her lilting soprano voice humming an unrecognizable tune and then adding words to the melody. *"Abide with me; fast falls the eventide; the darkness deepens, Lord with me abide; when other helpers fail and comforts flee; Help of the helpless, O abide with me."* I hum along as I wander toward the parlor and stretch out on the only couch, falling quickly into a deep sleep.

I must have been out only an hour or so when I am awakened by a nurse tapping on my shoulder. "He's gone, right?" I say, sitting up and trying to focus.

"Yes," she answers, her voice low and without animation.

"How's Joan?" I ask.

"I'm just heading down there. Thought you might want to join me." My heart pounds as the sound of our footsteps heralds our coming. We approach the door and peek into the darkness. As my eyes adjust, I see two people enveloped in each other's arms. Moving slowly toward her, I bend down and whisper, "Erik's gone."

"I know, dear," she answers.

"I'll just be outside the door then," I say, getting the impression that she is not quite ready to let go. "Let me know when you need me."

Since she had wished for candles earlier, I run off to the kitchen to find some. There are votives in the cupboard and matches by the gas stove. I rush back with my hands full, feeling better prepared now with the accoutrements for ritual, and sit Indian style on the floor to be there if she calls.

A few hours later, she opens the door, dressed once again in her comfortable daytime clothes, and invites me in. Erik appears as he did when I last saw him—in a deep sleep. "I found some candles, Joanie. Would you like me to light them?"

"That would be perfect." As the darkened room begins

to glow we sit down, each in her private world, until she breaks the silence. "As I told you, dear, I've never experienced anything like this before. I have no precedent to follow."

"Perhaps we are meant to keep the focus on Erik, to think and talk about him. You've brought so many of his favorite things to the room and he lived so many roles."

Her eyes are on fire, glistening now with tears that come not from sadness but from rich remembrances.

"You know, they'll ask at the funeral home for information about him. Should I take some notes while you talk?"

And so, as the dark night gives way to the dawn, she reflects on a life well lived, speaking of all the places and events that made them such a vibrant partnership—their meeting in Vienna, escaping to Denmark, then on to the United States, and eventually to Cambridge and teaching at Harvard. She describes his work with the Native Americans, and then his study of Gandhi, Martin Luther, and more. To say that he or they "made the most of their dash" would be an understatement.

Our reverie is disrupted with a knock at the door. "It is time, Mrs. Erikson," the night nurse informs her. We exit the room as they prepare to remove Erik. Minutes later he is whisked off and we follow closely behind.

"There should be a bugle or something, don't you think?" she asks.

I swallow hard. Oh, what I would give for a magic wand. Empty-handed, we simply wave the hearse away.

"Joanie, we can continue on, you know. Would you like to go with Erik to the funeral home?"

She nods. We head quickly to my car. Her need to have a ceremonial ending is obvious. "How can one's life be so meaningful for so long and then suddenly, poof, it's over with so little fanfare?" she says, with sudden gloom.

"Perhaps because you always stayed in the present, never even contemplating this day. Living has always been more important to you, and I daresay to Erik, than dying. It was a perfect evening. You did have it just the way you wanted it, didn't you?

"Yes, dear, I did," she sighs.

It is almost too much to grasp, and yet I will always be able to assure her that she surely made the most of it.

CHAPTER NINE

JOY IS A DUTY

I t's fall, and I've all but lost track of Joan since Erik's death and subsequent memorial service. She has been wavering between two personas—that of a dignified woman who receives the numerous visitors flooding her house to express their condolences, and that of a recluse. The public Joan who is mourning has no time for sustained, intimate conversation; the private, grief-stricken Joan stays put in her emotional wilderness, reliving her special and private memories alone.

Although I respect her need to grieve on her own terms, I sense she should have a bit of diversion to ease her out of her grief. It was she who told me that she didn't hit bottom awfully easily. "When I do," she once admitted, "I try to focus, not on the problem but on my strength. One way out of the doldrums is to do something . . . take action rather than sit passively."

And then one day she left a message on my machine, her normally melodic voice sounding desperate: "I feel suddenly left out of what must be going on around me. Please, dear, call and let me in on the action." I raced out of the house and headed for the beach. This being a foggy day—her favorite beach weather—I thought I might find her there. Sure enough, I spot her black cape billowing in the wind as she walks along the shore.

"Joanie," I shout, waving fiercely in hopes that she will notice my arrival. "May I join you?"

She turns slowly, then lifts her cane. I race to her side and gather her fragile body into my arms. "How are you?" I whisper. "It's been a while."

"All right until you asked me in that sympathetic tone. I guess I'm coping, but I hurt down to the bones," she says, as tears fill her eyes.

I pull back and stare at her absent look while she dabs a tear with an already dampened handkerchief.

"It's all right, Joanie," I say. "You've told me so many times that the way to feel a whole range of emotions is to use them. Well then, why are you holding back now? A most enormous event has occurred in your life. You need to dive into the emotion of it."

"But I've been doing this too much, lately. I can't cry forever, now, can I? How pitiful would that be?"

I reach out to offer another caress and she falls into my embrace and sobs unabashedly.

"Cry," I say, as her shoulders shake with emotion. "You must go through some things crying all the way if you're ever going to live with them without crying."

"What was that?" she asks, suddenly straightening up her body.

"A quote from Howard Thurman. It makes sense, doesn't it?"

"It really does," she agrees, swallowing her tears and now gazing at the endless sea. We stand in silence until she reaches for my hand and we plow on through the damp, mushy sand, listening to the honking gulls and the distant foghorn.

"Quite a fog," I suggest. "Perhaps it will melt your grief."

"Makes you lean on your senses, that's for sure. I keep telling myself that I can be either powerful like the sea or as weak as the broken shells under our feet. Of course you know which I'd prefer." She bends over to pick up a cluster of orange and yellow jingle shells that sparkle in her palm, and then drops them into her skirt pocket. "I think that I'm meant to create a new dimension out of Erik's and my love."

"What do you mean?" I ask gently.

"Maybe I'm meant to finish the stages," she answers, abstractly.

"I thought they were long finished," I say, puzzled.

"The eighth stage could stand some revising. Erik and I wrote about old age long before we were there," she says with a chuckle. "And now I'm finding that there is another stage or two beyond the eighth. I've been pondering the extension of the life cycles, especially since I'm finally in the last stages and more aware than ever of what they mean," she says, with a certain alacrity in her voice and posture that I haven't seen for some time. "I just need to make the latter stages understandable for others. And it would be a way to honor Erik's work and our life together."

I can hear the wheels turn as she ponders the idea. More importantly, I can see a new strength creeping into her stride, as if her imagination has refired her entire being. Just as I am about to ask her to elaborate she turns her gaze on me.

"What brings you out here today, anyway?" she asks, looking puzzled. "I mean, I may like the fog but it isn't your favorite thing."

"I came with an invitation."

"For me? Sounds intriguing."

"I'm glad you think so, because a few friends are arriving from New York tonight. I'm anxious to show them a good time. Each of them has been dealing with big issues and they need a chance to let the air blow through their lives. You'd be such a tonic for them. They've heard me talk about you and they're hoping you might join us for some of our activities."

"Such as?"

"Well, a seal watch, for one. I've been wanting to take you out to South Beach for months and this seems to be the perfect opportunity. How about it?"

"Your timing is impeccable, dear," she says, her eyes suddenly alive. "Getting out in a boat and doing something wild should wake me up, don't you think?"

"So we're on?"

"Damn right," she answers, eager to yield. I'm relieved, both because I feel that I guessed right in reaching out to her, and because my friends will only benefit from being around such a wise old woman. "I've got a list of things to accomplish before tonight. Can I give you a lift back to your house?" I ask her.

"That would be lovely, dear."

Dawn came early. My friends had arrived quite late. But since we hadn't seen one another for over a year it wasn't enough to have one glass of wine and go to bed. There was some major catching up to do. Hazel had switched jobs and moved to a house that needed to be completely reno-vated; Judy's husband had died, leaving her to run the fam-ily business; and Martha had the sad job of helping her son-in-law die while also being supportive to her daughter and grandchildren. To say any of us was resting on her lau-rels would be ridiculous. Rather, we were all attempting to stay afloat, and this weekend was meant to be a tonic if not a temporary cure.

I head for the kitchen to warm up some homemade scones and put on the coffee. With so few walls in the cot-tage, merely walking through it is enough to arouse even the deepest of sleepers. Sure enough, one after another stumbles into the kitchen shortly after six. "You promise this is worth it," Judy quips, rubbing her eyes and stagger-ing toward the coffeepot. "I've never been an early riser, and after the stress of last year I am sleep deprived."

"You told me you wanted to taste a bit of my life, didn't you? The mornings are the best time here. Besides, I have so much to introduce you to and not enough time in a mere weekend to do it. I trust you slept well—you did get a good seven hours, after all."

"Like a rock...how could I not have? That loft re-minds me of a tree house."

"Do we need our slickers?" Hazel asks, emerging from her quarters on the porch, already impatient to get going.

"Just lots of layers. The ride out will be windy and cool, but once we drop anchor, you'll want to bask along with the seals."

"You're not exactly roughing it like I imagined," Judy says as she looks up toward the cathedral ceiling. "I mean, these are pretty nifty digs."

"It was humble before Robin got involved. I'll blame him for dressing it up."

Martha is the last to present herself, and before long the counter is crowded with everyone involved in her breakfast routine—segmenting grapefruit, toasting bread, scrambling eggs, steaming milk, and brewing tea.

I pull away from the action and gaze at my friends, realizing how much I need more female companionship. "I've missed you guys," I say, plopping myself down at the table with a mug of coffee, all misty-eyed, seeing just now that even though the distance of our lives has become huge, the gap between our hearts remains small. "Thanks for coming."

"Hell, we needed to see if you were all right," Hazel pipes up. "And to understand why you left us behind."

"You look different," Martha says. "I can't quite put my finger on it."

"It's probably the tan. I have it year-round now because I'm rarely inside."

"No, it's more than that," Martha continues. She's the philosopher among us, always probing, searching beneath the surface of things. "There's a serenity. For one thing, you don't wrinkle your brow like you used to."

"Maybe that's because she's no longer angry," Hazel guesses. "When you left there was no talking to you—no rationalizing anything. I thought you were to become just another angry feminist."

"Really? I think women become angry and aggressive not because they're feminists but because they're on empty— they've lost all connection to themselves, to their feminine energy," I argue.

"I buy that," Judy says. "Losing David and becoming part of the male world has made me lose touch. I already feel different just breathing the sea air and hiding in your woods."

"One thing I've learned is that when you can no longer get in touch with your instinct and intuition, it's all over. I can't believe what you've all been through this past year. You've all got to be on automatic as well as on empty. I hope the Cape can bless you as it has me."

"Well, then, let's get going," Hazel shouts, pouring what's left of the coffee into a thermos and loading her backpack with scones and muffins. "It's six forty-five and counting."

We all pile into Judy's van. "Which way?" she asks, bringing me to attention.

"Take a right toward town. We're picking up Joan Erikson."

"Who?" Judy asks.

"Joan's new old friend," Hazel says. "I met her when I came to visit last winter. She's a goddess, really, more than ninety years old and seemingly indefatigable. Wait until you meet her."

I point out the local landmarks as we creep along the empty streets—the library, village green, newsstand, hardware store, and, of course, the church, before turning right onto Parallel Street and into Joan's driveway. She is ready and waiting, eager as a seven-year-old on her first day of school, dressed for action in sensible black sneakers, a windbreaker she bought at the church thrift shop, and a woolen hat pulled over her ears.

"You must have been joking," Martha says, peering over her half frames in awe. "She couldn't be ninety something."

"Ninety-two, to be precise," I say. "You're in for a treat."

"Well, hello, everyone," she says in her most melodic voice, attempting to make eye contact with each woman before buckling her seat belt. "It's awfully nice of you to include me. I could barely sleep a wink last night. Joan has talked so much about the seals, I can't believe I'm finally going to visit them."

"What's the big deal about seals?" Judy wonders.

"I guess you could say they've become my totem," I say.

"Your what?" Hazel asks.

"I have gotten a new lease on life by just walking these shores and hanging out with creatures instead of people. Once you gaze into the dark pool of a seal's eyes you will never be the same. I blame a lot of this on Joanie here," I say, patting her knee. "She keeps telling me I have to get out of my head and into my body."

"I'm not sure, dear," she answers. "I think it's the other way around. You've been the one to get me out and onto the beaches every day."

"But how did you get into seals?" Hazel probes.

"I ran into a bunch of fishermen at a local hangout and overheard them talking about the invasion of seals on South Beach and Monomoy. The idea of such creatures being in the surrounding waters was beyond intriguing. I just came right out and asked one of them if he'd take me out to see them. It was a real turn-on."

"That's not all that turned you on," Hazel continues. "You've mentioned that fisherman more than once. Are you sure it's the seals that made you wild and salty?"

"Oh, Hazel, you do have a way of bringing everything down to its lowest common denominator."

"Well?" Hazel continues, with an impish grin.

"I didn't sleep with him, if that's what you mean."

"Pity," Hazel says. "That would have been a delicious discussion to begin our weekend. An affair on the flats."

"So much for propriety and being on your best behavior in front of my new friend," I exclaim.

"Don't censor your thoughts on account of me," Joan insists. "I love it. Besides it's a nice distraction from doom and gloom."

"Yeah, I knew we could be ourselves in front of you," Hazel says, squeezing Joan's shoulder.

"The point is to be less serious," Joan says, "and more playful. Children have it right—that is, until someone knocks sense into them and the life out of them. I always insist that joy is a duty."

We are winding our way down Old Comers, an untraveled road where ponds and forests rule, until the sea faces us with its huge breakers rolling in from the Atlantic. We pass the fish pier, several old rambling homes, and eventually come to the lighthouse, where the road drops down to sea level. We inch our way down a single lane paved with seashells toward the marina, where forty or fifty boats are lined up in their little slips, and the pungent smell of drying seaweed affirms that we have arrived.

"Which boat's for us?" Joan asks, hopping out, cane in hand. I point toward the dock and gangplank and off she goes. The others follow, not nearly as eager, and climb aboard to find Joan already at the bow clasping the railing.

As our captain, Pete, starts up the motor and backs away from the dock, I can feel their excitement, even though they have no idea what is ahead of them. For now, time has stopped. There is nothing reasonable or practical about our little adventure, which makes it all the more appealing. As we creep out of the harbor, we feast our eyes on blue herons standing majestically in tall grasses, a female osprey tending her nest high atop an old telephone pole, the orange sun coloring the flats, and the clammers who labor there.

"I want to be nature," Joan exclaims.

"You mean you want to be in nature, right? You'll get that on this excursion, that's for sure."

"No, dear, I said I want to *be* nature—you know, unblemished, natural, primitive, even," she corrects me. "That makes all the difference."

"Well, don't feel you have to jump overboard to do so," I quip. "And once we pick up speed, you might be more comfortable sitting down."

"Thank you, Mommy," she says sarcastically, reluctantly taking a seat just as the engine is cranked to full throttle. The boat skims across the top of the water and pushes against the current. We are wind tossed, salt sprayed, and utterly at home in the glory of the ride. I glance back at the wake, which I usually miss, being so conditioned to look ahead, and see the frothy turbulence that always invigorates me. We travel around buoys, lobster pots, sandbars, and a few other vessels. After a time I begin looking for seals, spotting one or two whose heads bob as we speed by and then disappear just as fast. Just when I begin to worry that perhaps they have migrated on to some other place, I spot a cluster of them far off in the distance, the beach now a stretch of brown, gray, and white.

"There they are," I point, and all heads turn as the captain cuts back on his engine so we can begin to glide closer. It has been said that seals, more than any other animal, have a dreamlike effect on the human mind, and so it appears as I peer around at my friends—faces suddenly unlined and smooth, eyes wide open, eager to digest impressions.

Several seals raise their heads, look at us with mild interest, let off a snuffle or two, and then huddle back down with one another. "Oh, to be a seal," Hazel whispers, clearly entranced. Joan has long since risen from her seat and is kneeling now, half spread over the bow.

"'Web-footed seals forsake the stormy swell,'" Joan sings, "'and sleep in herds, exhaling nauseous smells.' That's from Homer, I think. Never thought I'd get to see such a thing." With that she further drapes herself over the bow of the boat and commences to howl, first letting out a guttural sound, followed by a hoot, and then the howl again as if she knows their language. Sure enough, she makes contact. One seal, then another, tumble into the water until the entire lot of them are in the sea, not swimming but treading water, their eyes fixed on us and our little boat. Suddenly, a massive bull, lounging somewhat away from the shoreline, lets out a roar, perhaps warning the colony of impending danger, which sends fifty or more into the water, where they have more control over their destiny.

We are speechless and watch as the dance begins. They begin gliding like a corps de ballet, some lured by silvery clouds of fish, others by Joanie's continued howls, leaping out of the water with arched backs and then diving down into the deep, dark bottom, leaving only a trail of bubbles behind.

"Where are they?" Martha wonders as we look around in every direction for signs of them.

Splash! Several surface at the bow, several more at the stern, and eventually we are surrounded, utterly delighted as the magic of the moment coexists so wonderfully with actual reality. Seeing the grace with which they move is like watching a spirit come alive. Although they are alert, the seals remain comfortable, gentle creatures, curious, vulnerable, and more trusting than they should be.

"Oh, to swim like that," Judy says, "and to be so at home in my body. I have such disdain for mine."

"I was just thinking the same thing," I say. "If only we could spread our wings and be freer with our bodies, we too could lighten up and recharge our souls."

"Do you think they are inviting us in?" Martha wonders. "That look they give you before diving under? I think it's an invitation."

About twenty of them have drifted off toward the gentle surf that has picked up. They are riding the waves, happily doing somersaults in the action. As we watch in awe, a baby seal appears right beside the boat, popping its head out and staring straight at Joan—its little whiskers twitching, its eyes as big as golf balls. And then, having made contact, it dives under again, the clear water permitting us to watch as it swims down to the bottom.

"Wow!" Joan sighs and then, somewhat overcome,

plops down on her seat. "I've had my moment—all the nourishment I can handle for today." Her grief has all but disappeared.

And then with a jolt Pete turns on the ignition. Our time in paradise is over. Although it is always hard for me to leave such a place behind, I can see from the satisfied faces that everyone is more than fulfilled. Besides, the seals seem to have lost their interest in us and have scattered in various directions—some back onshore rubbing and twisting their plump bodies in the sand before rolling over and basking in the warm sun; others, off to fish; and a pod of twenty or so is heading out to sea.

We sit in silence, letting our senses ferment, as Pete turns the boat around and heads back to town. Several seals follow in our wake and then disappear for good. I am struck by their medial nature—the ability to go from one world to another, being fully and unabashedly alive in both. As I look at the serenity on my friends' faces, grief is momentarily gone, and in its place is well-deserved peace and contentment.

Too soon we are back in port. It is always a shock.

"Where have we been?" Hazel asks, as we stagger up the gangplank and head for the van.

"Somewhere far away," Judy answers dreamily.

"I'm not sure I want to go anywhere," Martha says. "It seems too radical a move."

"I know," I say. "I feel that each time, but never fear, I won't let the spell be broken. There's more of the same as long as the weather holds." Reluctantly, everyone piles into the van and we're off.

"Weren't they like children?" Joan asks. "Those creatures have made me be playful again."

"Hear, hear." Judy agrees. "Something I must make more time for."

"That's it," I think aloud. "That's why I never want to return to shore after a time out there. Drifting around, away from structure, experiencing wildness only make me want more. It's a tightly strung world we are made to inhabit."

"Indeed," Joanie affirms. "But now we have an image with which to work. Like the seals, we don't have to have a whole batch of knowledge. We have a whole lot of senses to pay attention to. They'll tell us how to behave."

"Seal sense, I call it. It's seems we've all gotten a dose of it," I say, coining a new term that seems to fit our new awareness.

I rest my head back against the seat and feel so blessed that I could share this time and place. Once again, by leaving the safety of shore we have transcended our individual hurts. The motion and emotion of our little voyage has taken away the pain. What's more, our thinking has dissolved into just being. We have abandoned all things rigid and will breathe freely for a time.

CHAPTER TEN

THOUGHTS OF A LIFE
WELL DIGESTED

J oan is her old self again—well, almost. It's not that she is anesthetizing her grief, but she's transcending it by taking action rather than dwelling in sadness. Her muted and clouded glances are being replaced by eyes bright and piercing as she works away on some of Erik's unpublished and unfinished manuscripts, her prime objective being to revise the eighth stage of the life cycle and add a ninth stage as well.

To ensure her success she has imported her old secretary from somewhere in the Midwest, rented a computer, and turned her little house into a bustling office. "I'm ninety-three," she explained, "not retired, serene, or gracious, and I'm eager to figure out these final stages before it is too much of an undertaking." As usual, she wants to make sure that I am equally productive, prodding me to develop essays about my year alone. Implied, of course, in her nudging is always the idea that we're meant to have experiences and then share them. "It's not about you, dear. It's about being generative and giving back. In a sense you are privileged to have had a cottage to run to as well as a portable career to bring along. I saw how you talked with your friends and how they responded. Can't you see how people are sick for the truth? Nothing in our culture encourages us to break out of the mold. Since you did just that, you must have volumes to talk about."

Easy for her to say! She has spent a lifetime pondering her development while I'm only just beginning to experiment. Putting words to my solitary year, whose meaning is still unresolved in my mind, is proving difficult. I sit in my spartan upstairs office, tapping my pencil against the desktop, while she produces pages of theory each day for her secretary to type up each afternoon. To say I'm intimidated would be an understatement. Having spent most of my writing life focusing on others, I find that shifting direction now to tell my story in the first person is absolute hell.

When not staring off into space, my eyes settle on a rather playful Chagall print, which dangles precariously from a hook not far from the desk, put there on purpose by Joan, no doubt, for times like this when humor and playfulness elude me. She has also tacked a quote of Erik's on the wall above the desk: *There are certain individuals who, in the process of resolving their own inner conflicts, become paradigms for broader groups."*

The only other helpful object that lives with me in this isolated world is an electronic typewriter, purchased at the church thrift shop. "We'll each work through the morning," she said all eager and with great intention, "and then share what we've accomplished over lunch, remaining loose and free, dear, enjoying the freshness of each other's ideas. I'm so thrilled to have someone in my daily life with whom I can expand."

It was this last comment that almost sent me packing. It's one thing to talk about the craft of writing and the importance of harnessing fresh thoughts, and quite another to produce material on cue—readable stuff that might send her to another level. So I sit and doodle, then stand and look out the window, then sit and jot down a cluster of related thoughts, then walk off to another room and lose myself in books she has stashed in a floor-to-ceiling bookcase, all the while knowing that I have wasted the best time of my writing day—the morning—when the mind has yet to click in and when distractions are no more than dreams. Mercifully, the clock strikes one and I'm off to prepare our lunch.

As I busy myself mixing up a can of tuna with as many vegetables as she has on hand, I feel as anxious as a student who hasn't completed her homework assignment. And yet, Joan hasn't put herself in the role as taskmaster. It's my damn ego again, telling me I want to be more than I am or seem. Why not just fess up and see what she can do to help? Haven't I watched many a writer appear on her doorstep in search of advice?

As we slurp soup out of pottery bowls she made years ago, the inevitable question comes up: "So, dear, how's it going? What have you to read to me? I'm dying to know the direction your thoughts are taking you."

I waste no time getting my despair onto the table. "Sorry to say, I've hit a wall. The only thing that I've come up with in over a week is a theme—ebb tide. When I ran away, I felt as though I was in that tide—not coming or going, just being circular. Unfortunately, after a year of virtual meditation and reflections I'm ashamed to say that clarity still eludes me and I remain as circular as the ebbing tide. In any case, I can't put my evolvement into words."

"You've got a beginning," Joan responds, full of encouragement. "Actually, you've got more than that—a concept, no less, and a good one. This process takes time. You emerge slowly when you truly listen to your heart. There's no putting a time frame on soul work."

Her sympathy and encouragement relieves me. Why was I even the slightest bit nervous? I bite into my sandwich reinvigorated for the moment.

"I often need to remind myself of this too, when I'm forcing thoughts. That's why I have Mark Van Doren's poem on my desk," she says, quoting a few lines:

Slowly wisdom gathers
Golden dust in the afternoon
Somewhere between the sun and me
Sometimes so near that I can see it
Yet never settling late or soon.

"Apropos, isn't it?"

"For you, perhaps, but I'm not one of those people who does well waiting for things to slowly gather. Besides, I'm having another, more technical problem with my writing."

"What's that, dear?"

"I find it impossible to use the *I* word. I mean, who cares what I have to say? I'm not well known as you are. In fact I'm somewhat of a nobody."

"Well, you are someone who has departed from the norm, that's for sure. But, I must say that I'm not at all surprised that you are having trouble writing about yourself.

It's a habit I've noticed in all of your social interactions. You tend to please yourself by giving others the stage, keeping your opinions at arm's length to avoid conflict, thus leaving yourself totally out of the process."

"So what do I do about it?"

"You've already begun, whether you know it or not, by pursuing so many unanswerable questions with a like-minded friend."

"In a way our conversations seem like a cheat. We talk, I learn, but then those thoughts sink into my consciousness and so far haven't found their way onto paper."

"Look, dear, you are in a generative time of life and doing a damn good job of staring reality in the face. Now, the opposite of generativity is stagnation. Yuck! The word alone should get you off the dime."

"But how exactly do I get out of my head and into my body? That is the question!"

"It's difficult to create a dividing line between thoughts and feelings, but it would behoove you to at least start honoring your feeling life more than you do."

"So?" I continue to probe as she seems to be coming up with thoughts I can take hold of.

"Adventure gets you to a feeling level and keeps the mind at bay. Allow your imagination and feelings to follow whatever image moves you. Don't you remember when we came upon that red fox staring into a puddle?"

I smile at the memory.

"We came away from that moment realizing the importance of reflection. If I recall we spent the rest of the afternoon reflecting on reflection. It's a matter of using all that is around you, merging your senses with the world like an animal or child would do to find the clarity you seek. Once again, the key is to loosen up. Where curiosity and playful discovery are the focus of activity, there's little opportunity to fail."

"There you go again with your thoughts about taking action."

"Damn right. Ideas do not germinate when you simply sit inside and stare at a piece of paper. You need to activate them again and again—bring it all to life."

Her words are encouraging, but writing personal essays seems, more than ever, like an uphill battle.

"And for God's sake," she says, now sounding like a coach or a cheerleader, "take off that woolen skirt you wear all the time, tie a piece of chiffon around your waist, get rid of your underpants, and go sit in the sand for a while. You'll recover your feelings and ideas in no time." She twinkles, laughing at her own counsel. "After all, wisdom comes from life's experiences well digested. Stop relying so much on your mind and get in touch with experience."

"Okay. Okay. I hear you. Enough about me. I've got the picture. Let's finish up lunch so that I can get on with it and you can get back to your secretary. Overhearing your babble as you dictate to her or into your tape recorder, I am more than curious as to where your thoughts are taking you."

"I've got a ways to go, but what's coming up is very surprising. When Erik and I deemed that wisdom and integrity were the strengths of old age, we were a bit off the mark."

"Really?"

"Yep. Those words were simply too exalted and indefinable. I'm beginning to see that I must bring them down to actuality in order to make the eighth stage more credible."

"I like that idea," I say, "because you really are demonstrating to me that it is never too late to pick up a lost stitch or revise yourself."

"Good, dear, I'm so grateful for that affirmation. Anyway, I've been digging deep into such places as the *Oxford Dictionary* and Sanskrit to find some initial clues. Wisdom, in the end, comes from the word *veda,* which means 'to see' and 'to know.' Isn't that fun?"

"You mean it has nothing to do with knowledge?"

"Quite the contrary. It's simply about seeing. And integrity, it turns out, is about tact, which means touching! Seeing and touching. Back to the senses again. That's what older people have been doing their whole life through. So it seems obvious that no matter who you are, once you get to the eighth stage, you've lived your wisdom. Anyway, that's a roundabout way of telling you that I have major revisions to do before going on to the ninth stage. Good thing I'm having fun with it, isn't it?"

"That's for sure. I've always found revising to be a drag," I say.

"I can't allow anything to slow me down now. My clock is ticking. I've arrived, so to speak—don't have all the time in the world, you know." Although she's cavalier about growing older, I hear a tinge of sadness in her voice as her eyes cloud over.

"You're always thinking about that dash, aren't you?" I say, which snaps her back to attention.

"Indeed. Look, I know we have it in us. Having been solitary children, you and me, we were shaped to be writers. When you've been on the outside from the beginning you become a keen observer."

"I never thought that a benefit would come from loneliness."

"Well, in my case, contemplative writing (and that's what you're about to do), is neither clever nor literary. Instead, it accurately records what one observes inside and out."

I clear the dishes and rinse them off, needing to move about and be busy. Her continued pep talk is making me itchy. "Would you like a cup of tea?" I ask, interrupting her train of thought.

"That would be lovely, dear ... and there are some cookies in the cupboard we might like to have."

Although I continue to busy myself with incidental chores, she is relentless. "You know what I think? I think you're afraid to actually put into words the rules you broke, how you broke them, and what the aftermath really feels like—how much of it you've enjoyed but how much remains unresolved."

She's right again. There she goes, stirring the warring nation within me. I suppose I'm ambivalent about what I did and just who I've become as a result. I'm feeling strained relations with my own immediate past. So many truths I don't want to admit even now, and God knows, I don't want to see them in print. My silence must be telling her that she's hit a chord.

"Henry James said that a writer must be willing to embarrass himself," she continues, without finger-wagging, but sounding like a lawyer, sealing up her case. "Everyone wants to hear the voice of someone who has gone through something real. I think that's you," she says, resting her case and getting up from the table. "C'mon, follow me. We're going into my bedroom to rummage through my cedar chest."

"For a piece of chiffon?" I quip.

"Something better," she says with a mischievous wink.

Pulling chairs up and sitting beside a mahogany coffin-like box, she lifts up the top. "My treasures," she says, pointing to a jewelry box with some of her handcrafted necklaces, several wood carvings, which Erik made when he was an artist, and beneath, piles of exotic outfits—saris bought during her time in India, capes that she designed, magnificent silk and woolen scarves, and down toward the bottom, the piece of fabric she was looking for. "Here it is," she says, pulling it out and holding it up. "A sarong. I can't remember where I got it. It is so you with all the fish and sea life scattered across the silk—perfect for a Pisces! You'll look smashing. What's more, you'll feel free!"

"I'm meant to wear this?" I say, tentatively.

"Yep, and the less underneath the better. Underclothes are such an enslavement, especially when you're young. I wear as few as possible. Time to get your body in line with your mind, dear. You won't feel dead after a time, I promise. Just get out there and skip."

She has tried every treatment and trick to coax some newness out of me, urging me to believe in myself. "You may just have to become somebody you never intended," she says, as we make our way back to the kitchen. "Retrace your steps, revisit those bogs, beaches, and marshlands where the echoes of your thoughts rise and fall with the tides. It's time you take your own prescriptions."

She seems eager to get back to work now that she has offered me a charge—to feel my way back through experience. "Oh, take this along with you," she adds. "I bought it at a craft fair not long ago . . . isn't it gorgeous? The artist bound this book herself, and the pages are parchment. I think it's perfect for you as you begin to become more transparent. See you in a few days."

And with that, I am out the door, ready to try writing her way, touching and absorbing the moments that will make me truer to myself, and give me some substance to pass on.

CHAPTER ELEVEN

PRACTICE NONSENSE

With nose to the grindstone I spend the next few months discovering and rediscovering myself and actually getting it down on paper. That is, until I received a phone call from my cousin asking me to accompany her and her husband to Peru. "We're going to hike the Inca Trail," she said, more than excited about the possibility. "Want to come along?" I felt the stirrings of my old nomad spirit. It would certainly be a welcome break from my writing, I reasoned, or perhaps such an adventure would add a new dimension to my work. Yet, there were trepidations.

"Do you think we're up to it?" I asked her. "After all, we're not kids, you know."

"That's the point," she countered. "It's now or never. You're the one who's always lecturing me about living our unlived lives."

"Okay. Okay. Give me twenty-four hours to deliberate." Of course, I no sooner get off the phone with my cousin than I get back on to consult with Joan.

"There's no question," she says, without the slightest hesitation. "You must go. It's one thing to hazard out in a safe place and another in unknown territory. Taking chances and risking routine are two important ingredients for keeping alive. Besides, a new panorama always offers fresh insight."

"I thought you'd approve, but the practical side of me wonders if I can afford it. And really, am I just running away again, trying to avoid reality?"

"In a setting such as Machu Picchu? I shouldn't think so! It'll be a chancy thing, what with the altitude and all, but when an opportunity such as this presents itself, you need to grab it."

"Thanks for your blessing. Now all I need to do is ask Robin. He may not be so thrilled."

"No more asking permission," she says, almost jumping through the phone. "Whose life is it anyhow? You didn't ask if you could run to the Cape, did you? Erik and I were often going off in separate directions in pursuit of one goal or another. Besides, haven't you learned by now that no one ever pushes you toward freedom. You need to take that for yourself."

"Well, I guess then, I'm off to Peru!"

"Sounds likely," she says, "but before you take off, I suggest you make friends with your body. It's the only vessel you'll have to help you along."

Her comment is sobering.

"How many weeks before you leave?"

"Eight," I answer.

"Good. That should give us ample time to plot out an exercise program. You're a bit too solid ... could do with some loosening up. As a matter of fact, you don't look stretched."

"What?" Her directness hurt.

"It's as if you haven't gotten out of maternity."

"Am I to take that to mean that you think I'm fat?"

"No dear, just a little unused. Life can go pretty dull when you don't take care of your machine, and I'm afraid yours needs a bit of an overhaul."

"You didn't actually think that I'd go off on such a rigorous adventure without training, did you?" I ask indignantly, taking her constructive criticism badly.

"You'll need to do more than bike or walk," she insisted. "You wouldn't want to lose your grit in the middle of the trek, would you?"

"Of course not. So what are you suggesting?"

"Well, there's always my treadmill, and then I'd have you do my porch steps with a loaded pack on your back—

say, ten times in a row, and if we add weights to your walks you should be fit in no time."

All summer long she worked me hard during the weeks before my trip, and just now, as I gaze at the towering Andes that surround me, I'm grateful for her push as well as her encouragement. "You must have confidence in your body. It's a portable world—a wonder, really. It will get you through anything if you take care of it."

Still, as I sit here on a boulder beside the Urubamba River and watch the porters rearrange our gear so that it will fit snugly over their backs, I feel nervous and wonder why I thought I was up to this challenge in the first place. Perhaps a problem will occur that might force us to postpone or even cancel the trek, I find myself hoping.

A cool breeze brushes the sweat of apprehension from my brow, and I suck in the energy that comes from the rushing water. I am comforted by the motion and charge of the rapids as they splash over ancient rocks, all the while hoping that the sound will empower me up into the nearby hills. Andean women, colorfully dressed in oranges, purples, and reds, with bowler hats atop their heads, emerge from the surrounding hills and walk briskly to market, taking dainty pitter-patter steps as they balance bundles larger than our packs on their backs. *"Fuerte mujeras,"* Gustalvo says, pointing with pride at his country's strong women. I stiffen, ashamed at my laziness, and quickly begin gathering my water bottles and adjust my knapsack. There's no turning back now. I've taken the dare and have only Joan's wisdom to buoy me onward.

"Practice nonsense," she had shouted from her deck after handing me the yin/yang pendant that now hangs around my neck. "Have some joy during all your trudging, and don't forget to laugh. Tears no longer become you."

Remembering her words just now reminds me to relax my shoulders and do a few stretches before Gustalvo orders us onto the trail. *"Adelante!"* he shouts, barreling toward the hills, as he motions us to follow. My cousin and her husband comply with lightning speed, as I attempt to scurry up the first steep incline, panicked that I'll be left behind, but pretending courage, nonetheless. I feel like a tardy horse not yet at the starting gate although the race has begun. Will we always be moving so fast, even at the higher altitudes? Pushing hard now, my breathing becomes labored and my legs feel leaden. I continue for a few more minutes and then gasp, "Wait, wait up, please. I can't do this." As words of failure trickle out of my dry mouth, I see the end of this adventure before it has even begun.

My cousin backtracks, recognizing what I think must

be heart failure as merely a panic attack. "There's no need to hurry," she says, urging me to smell a handful of honeysuckle she has just picked. "Remember our pact? We would find our own pace. If this trek takes a week instead of four days, so be it." Her soothing words steady my breathing and allow me to regain some emotional momentum. As I take a swig of water, I feel my pulse slow.

Gustalvo, too, notices my anxiety and flushed face as he returns to check on us. "Don't push energy," he cautions, putting his arm around my shoulders. "Feel your body as you walk. Stop a little here and there. This trek is for you to connect with the earth . . . that is all."

I nod in agreement and feel momentarily reassured, allowing the elements to work their magic and unleash my senses. That's what Joan would prescribe. "See, smell, touch, and taste everything . . . that's what enlivens and links us in a sensuous way to the world outside ourselves. It's the very food we need for our body and soul."

I put one foot in front of the other and begin walking again, chanting aloud a line of Dag Hammarskjöld's: *"Be pure and dare in this fight with the mountain . . . with myself against me."* In a little while every gust of air brings with it one exotic scent after another. I soon pass the porters, who have stopped for water, and I move ahead. Perhaps by walking alone and not focusing on the others I won't be tempted to compete. Even so, this is a competition of sorts, not with anyone else but with myself—a private contract to be met. I'm here to test my endurance, independence, and potential. I begin to time my gait to the rushing rapids that echo up from the gorge below, all the while setting small goals: a promontory looming beyond a faraway bend; a mossy knoll in the distance; a ruin I spot on the map I carry in my vest pocket; an incline I intend to climb without stopping. Each goal asks something different from my body; each accomplishment creates a new sensation.

"Try to make your muscles do for you what your mind won't," Joan would say during our workouts, and so I do. I feel the tug of my flesh molding in response to gravity— to the earth beneath my feet, and just now I feel solidly grounded. Submerged in the tasks at hand, I am in the here and now, not missing the varied natural life that dots the trail. We trudge through muted desert dotted with red flowers that decorate the dullness, then lush jungle, and soon I'm scrambling up a sharp cliff.

I tiptoe over a rock slide, careful not to become part of its next precipitous collapse, then tread carefully along a narrow ledge to a log bridge that spans a bottomless canyon. I freeze. How do I negotiate this? I look for a detour, a way around, but there is none. I must go forward or stagnate, have faith or succumb to fear. I shuffle gingerly across the four feeble-looking logs, holding my breath until safe crossing is accomplished. Triumphs such as this prepare me for the next one.

Despite my growing confidence and a modicum of enjoyment, high adventure has its saturation point. After ten hours of steady walking I dream of a campfire, warm food, and snuggling inside a sleeping bag on some romantic peak. Just then a spattering of rain turns into a torrential downpour, and we take cover under a tree near a group of huts just off the instantaneously slippery trail. Gustalvo negotiates with the proprietor of a less-than-modest farm, asking permission for us to camp in his barnyard. This is something I hadn't bargained for—setting up a tent for the first time around animals and manure, with a Peruvian family standing by giving us their undivided attention. Lighting our stoves is out of the question. PowerBars and cereal with boxed milk poured on top will be the evening meal.

"It's the hard that makes it great," my son, the long-distance bicyclist, has told me. Just now I don't think so as I sink into silence in a corner of the tent. Yet stopping in such circumstances is a relief, and I soon begin to take advantage of even this respite. Tomorrow we climb into thinner air—13,730 feet—to Dead Woman's Pass, an ominous name that refuels my fears. I wonder how many people have actually died trying to cross over. Mercifully, my morbid thoughts melt away as the rhythmic spattering of rain hits all sides of the tent and lulls me to sleep.

I awaken early and quietly pack my gear, trying valiantly never to bring up the rear. As Gustalvo warns, the incline is steep from the onset, and I begin the climb feeling as if I am on an endless ladder. A lone stick lies across the path at this timberless altitude, and I quickly snatch it to use as a walking stick.

Ten steps, stop, breathe, then start again. I'm reduced to simply counting steps—no desire anymore to absorb the scenery. I'm pushing hard, wanting to get the ascent over with instead of relishing the cloud-shrouded mountains, wildflowers, and glacial lakes along the way. I had promised to stay in the moment and not just go for the goal, but now all I can think of is survival. "You must imagine your capacities," Joan had cautioned me, "how much strength you can muster, what you can do even before you set out. Then you will have the confidence to stretch yourself like never before."

For a time I make steady progress as the mechanics of my body kick in. Just as I think that wind is my only companion I pass several French students, but we don't speak—no one can spare the breath. We look like astronauts wandering about the moon in some sort of fog. One of their number has fallen ill with dysentery and is being hauled away on the back of a burro.

My temples begin to throb and my pulse quickens. I reach into my pocket for cocoa leaves, stuff them into my jowls, and suck, hoping to stave off further effects of the altitude. But as my breathing becomes shallow I sit down and look back to see my traveling companions doing the same.

Gustalvo feels we should stop, even though it is early afternoon. "It would be better to sleep low," he says, suggesting we retreat to further acclimate. The thought of backtracking is unthinkable, but I'm dizzy, nauseous, and ready for any suggestion. We set up camp on a wondrous plateau with a breathtaking 360-degree view of mountaintops and cloud formations, yet we succumb to sleep rather than admiring the sights. Hours later, when I awaken and delve into my backpack for snacks and a sweater, I find a list I'd made before the trip of all the reasons to do this trek, inspired by Joan's offhand remarks.

TAKE ACTION

HAVE ADVENTURES

FACE YOUR FEARS

SEIZE THE MOMENTS

TOLERATE ISOLATION

OVERDOSE ON THE SENSES

LEAN ON YOUR BODY

REACH BEYOND YOUR GRASP

When the sun set two hours ago, the sky went black for an instant and then, as if someone had plugged in a million twinkle lights, the mountainous world lit up. Now, I spread my body out on the floor of the tent and gaze through my little screen window at the ceiling of constellations while listening to Andean flute music being played by one of our porters. It was for all this and more that Joan pushed me forward.

Morning comes quickly and I head off before the others, refreshed from sleep, knowing of the task ahead. What's more, I have a newfound sense of respect for my old body: its muscles are expanding, stretching, working in sync with sockets and bone; my lungs are working nonstop like an accordion at a wedding reception; deep breathing has replaced shallow, quick gasping. My broad shoulders seem to welcome the heavy backpack as it pulls them back and straightens my spine. Suddenly and finally I seem to be commanding my space and feel "gloriously me," a term Joan coined about her early life as she was striving to be just that. The mountain allows me an hour or so of total well-being before my pace slows to a crawl once again, and my short-lived buoyancy diminishes. However, I'm determined not to have to retrace my steps. Struck by the fact that a good attitude always turns me around, I trudge on.

Several times I think the summit is near, but it is only an optical illusion—the top is never as close as it appears. Nonetheless, just seeing the ridge is bait enough. I am cloaked in clouds. The wind howls and the music of a narrow mountain stream breaks the eerie silence. I sense that each moment is both a beginning and an end, a small death and birth, never to be experienced again.

I am beginning to understand the myth of the phoenix—that magical bird that glided through these hills, eventually died, then rose again from its ashes, ever present still in this fertile land. Not only do the mountain people carry its freedom and strength with them as they wander the length of the Inca Trail but so do we pilgrims who come here seeking. Walking this trail, seeing this place is the difference between simply believing in the divine and knowing it. As I struggle with each breath, I make a silent promise to remember always to strive toward more unimaginable experiences.

After one more hour I haul my heavy body onto the summit—a near-frozen peak, barren but welcoming just the same. I gaze back at the long crooked line of trail in disbelief. I'm here, but once I was far away—down there. Pure grace alone has swept me up and over. I want to tarry, to relish the accomplishment. Euphoria sets in, especially since we are to travel downhill now on the famous steps of the Incas (all two thousand of them)—a marvel of construction.

But the air is chilling, and managing the tricky footwork of the descent is no easier than mastering the ascent, especially with trembling knees and weakened ankles.

Still, I'm thriving on motion and addicted to encountering the unexpected. Nothing can deter me—not a poisonous snake that slithers across my path (a sign of transcendence, Gustalvo says), not a dark slimy tunnel, not the final night's hike, during which, had it not been for the light of the full moon, we would have been lost in the mountains forever.

Then, as if I'm being awakened from a dream, the final day dawns and I feel surprisingly sad, not yet ready for the journey to end. "It won't be long now," Gustalvo says.

"The ancient city is within our grasp." Clumps of orchids, yellow flowering yucca, and spiny shrubs dot the last part of the trail, decorating the path as if for a homecoming. Soon I spot the Sun Gate in the distance, a stream of light shining through the archway, and I quicken my pace, impatient for a first look, wanting to be separate from the others.

It is a shock to come upon that which I've walked so far to claim—a bittersweet moment, even anticlimactic. But as the fog that so often hovers over Machu Picchu begins to lift, I feel the city draw me in. I proceed slowly now down high terraces and onto narrow cobbled lanes where llamas roam at will, and feel humbled.

This has been a journey of body and soul, an intimate experience between this land and me. I encounter a well-dressed Chilean woman who spots my walking stick and plies me with questions about the difficulty of the trail. Feeling momentarily full of myself, I answer her in my broken Spanish, leaving out the hard stuff, reporting the good, in hopes that she and others will tread where most dare not.

I continue, skipping down into sacred territory, wanting to retreat back into solitude, and begin to wander among stones that speak, soaking up what they have to say. No longer actively searching, I become simply a passive absorber. The sun has warmed the rock slab I choose to sit upon, and gradually it melts my aching body. I welcome the finish after so many fits and starts. If the trail is intended to be a learning place for emotions, than Machu Picchu seems to be the place to come to terms with them.

The Inca envisioned all things in duality—male and female, life and death, right and left, the upper world and the lower world. I see a pattern in the stones that reflect this premise, and I choose to stand in between the two tallest ones, my palms open, as I prepare for a quiet ritual that will honor the combined efforts of my mind and body. Perhaps I should remove Joan's pendant and leave it on the top of these stones. It was her spirit and push that got me here, a spirit that lives within me now. It is fitting to leave it here, I reason, and take it off, placing it in a small crevice in the main temple.

I rub my hands over the very smooth stones to remind myself to stay in touch. I have been leveled and grounded by intangibles—such things as endurance, patience, will, commitment—a pleasant combination of active and passive ingredients needed for harmony and balance. Sitting here and taking stock forces me to remember and cherish what it is to be vitally alive—somehow to transcend the mundane, to be broken and remade.

This city, created by ancients who revered all that was

true, natural, and real, is a place where the heavens align with the earth. No wonder I feel satisfied and safe, at home within myself. I've plateaued, but only long enough to catch my breath for the next summit. This journey is complete, but I feel as if my life once again has just begun.

CHAPTER TWELVE

HAPPILY GROUNDED

I sit safely cushioned, looking out the airplane window as the peaks of the Andes hastily disappear and leave me with just the memories of my challenging journey. Fortunately, flying suspends time and gives me a chance to break from one place before embracing another. It's a good thing, too, since I'm filled with emotions that need attention. This is not one of those moments when a job has been accomplished or a vacation has come to an end and I simply want to pack my bags and say next! This time I want to hold on to the messages of the mountain. It's difficult, though, in a crowded airplane, which has a culture of its own and insists the traveler be a part of it. "Good morning, ladies and gentlemen," says a voice from the cockpit. "We are heading east, over the Andes, and will soon be cruising at an altitude of thirty thousand feet. The wind is behind us and just now it appears that we will be landing in Boston a good twenty minutes ahead of schedule. Sit back, relax, and enjoy the flight."

I am trying to relax and slow down, but it's hard after weeks of perpetual motion. Joan told me that action and motion would conspire to take me to a new level, and this journey certainly was more about the body than the mind. I unfold my wrists, do a few neck rolls, stretch my legs as far as they will go under the seat in front of me, and sigh. This used to be a body that tried to be acceptable and hopefully pleasing to the eye. That's what mattered most. The fact that it contained me and two children, could give me sexual pleasure on occasion, and worked like a machine to keep me alive was immaterial. I never really thought about it with respect until this journey. Now I have a new understanding of the biblical metaphor of the body as a temple. In former times my body snagged and invalidated me, but right now it buoys and surprises me. I've given it a life of its own, lifting all restrictions, and in the process it is working far beyond my expectations.

I reach for a pillow and tuck it into the nape of my neck, then snuggle under a blanket and continue to gaze out the window at the billowing clouds. When Joan urged me to walk the Inca Trail, she insisted that by having a sense of potential, daring to pursue something, I eventually would win and feel empowered. "It happened when I went to Europe," she told me. "Setting a course, getting there, and then accomplishing what I set out to do—studying at all of the modern dance studios I could find, sealed my independence. In any case, richness of experience is a potential generator of wisdom."

Sigmund Freud thought that out of one's vulnerabilities comes strength. Is that the power that I suddenly feel—a new sense of strength? One thing I know for sure is that having escaped from my familiar world, I'm not eager to return to living quite so predictably. I want to remember to reach for the unknown or exotic as well as a measure of joy. "It's there for the taking," Joan constantly says, "and we must seize it for ourselves. The opposite of joy is shame and doubt. There's hardly any fun in that."

The flight attendant is serving breakfast and interrupts my train of thought. I devour the food in front of me—orange juice, coffee, cheese omelet, and sausage—quite a spread compared to the instant oatmeal, boxed milk, and granola bars we had on the trail. Still, there was a certain satisfaction in living the spartan life and dealing only with immediacies. I reach for the newspaper tucked in the seat pocket in front of me and quickly see that while I was away nothing earth-shattering has occurred. The same issues that were making news when I left home were still in the headlines upon my return. Do I need to clutter my mind with any of this right now? I quickly tuck the newspaper back where I found it, donning eye shades the minute my tray is removed in hopes of shutting out the busyness, wishing I could listen to Andean flute music and keep the spirit of South America alive. It occurs to me that in every life there are a few defining moments that seem to change the course we follow. I suspect that I have just had one of those moments. Slowly, exhaustion takes over, and I fall into a deep sleep.

When I awaken, we are plunging through the clouds on our way to land. I straighten up, run a brush through my tousled hair, and gather up my belongings—a gnarled walking stick, my journal, and several pieces of native art that would have been squashed in my duffel bag. Down below the quickly descending airplane, I see the prominent shoreline and the unmistakable arm of Cape Cod etched out of bubbling blue-green surf, and I smile. This very place embraced me when I was so desolate, and it now stands ready to welcome my triumph.

As we touch down and the plane comes to a screeching halt, most of the passengers jump up and reach into the overhead bins for their things. But I remain seated, a little saddened by the abruptness of the landing and reluctant to join the frenzy around me. Eventually, I disembark and make my way toward baggage claim. Still, I stand apart from the others, as if their high energy might spill over onto me. I spot my muddy backpack and worn duffel and then the limo driver, who ushers me out of the craziness and toward a revolving door.

The trip out to the Cape goes by much more quickly than usual, it seems. As we get closer I feel my adrenaline picking up again, not unlike the marathon runner who, after the finish line, massage, and shower, needs to relive the race. As we near town I ask to be dropped off at Joan's house. She doesn't respond to her chimes ringing, or to my rather bold knock. Is she there? More important, is she all right?

Just then, her housekeeper appears. "You're back," she says with a broad smile, dissolving my fears about Joan.

"Is she home?" I ask.

"No, she's gone for her walk—working out more these days. She's had a couple of fainting spells, and she's certain it's because she's been slacking off on her exercise. You'll probably find her up the street."

I drop my gear on the porch and hurry off, catching a glimpse of her slim figure about three blocks away. Curiously, she is sitting on a bench that I have never seen there before. I wave and call her name as she rises to greet me, holding out her arms in her usual welcoming gesture.

"Well, it's you. We meet again," she says, hugging me firmly. "It was awfully quiet without you around." I study her face, which is pale—the shimmering eyes are dull, and for a moment I feel somehow that I neglected her by going away.

"How are you? I hear you've had a couple of spells."

"Well, my body's been giving me some trouble. I conked out a few times. Imagine falling down, splat on the grass, right over there," she says, pointing with her cane, "and lying there for God knows how long with cars driving by and no one even thinking to stop. That's why I've built this bench. Isn't it sweet?" She is pleased with herself as she rubs her hand over the freshly varnished seat. "I had it constructed so others, like me, might have a place to fall!"

"Oh, Joanie, you amaze me."

"No, you amaze me, dear. Did you just blow in? You seem light as a feather."

"As a matter of fact, I haven't even been home yet—had the driver come straight to your house so we could talk before my impressions get watered down."

"I'm so glad you did," she says, as the color comes back into her cheeks. "I missed you."

"Well, I didn't miss you," I quip.

"Really?" she says, taken aback.

"No, silly, you were with me in spirit—every step of the way. I did leave your yin/yang pendant in a holy spot and brought you a stone in its place," I say, pulling it out of my pocket and placing it in the palm of her hand. "They speak, you know . . . the stones from Machu Picchu."

"You couldn't have given me anything better," she says. "This should keep me grounded. No more falling for me. You look absolutely bright, like a star or something." She is staring at me in a searching way.

"How about stretched? Do I look stretched?" I ask, standing up and turning around. "The journey was one continuous reach, let me tell you."

"Yes you do, as a matter of fact. I bet you're having trouble staying still," she guesses, grabbing her cane with one hand and me with the other. "Shall we walk?"

"I'd love to. The flight was dreadful—all cramped and constrained after being solo and free."

"So, tell me everything, from the moment you stepped off the plane."

"Phew! That's a tall order," I say, fumbling with the memories. "Where to start . . . it all seems pretty surreal just now. I would like to be able to say that when I get my photographs back it will all become vivid again. But my camera broke halfway through the first day and I was forced to commit everything to memory. I even drew some sketches of various sights along the trail."

"You finally had to depend on what you heard, saw, or smelled. Makes a difference, doesn't it?"

"That and walking at three miles per hour. The place was amazing. We trekked through every imaginable kind of landscape and the vegetation was dazzling—even wild orchids. I picked some wildflowers for you. They're drying in my journal. By the way, you don't happen to have any Peruvian relatives, do you?"

"Not as far as I know. Why do you ask?"

"The women there all have your attitude as well as your carriage, stamina, and the ability to walk endlessly! *Fuerte mujeras* is how our guide described them, which means strong woman in Spanish."

"You ought to be the one feeling strong today," she says, squeezing my hand to emphasize my accomplishment. "You did it! You actually walked the Inca Trail! No one can ever take that accomplishment away from you. That's one of the best reasons to take a journey."

"Could be," I say. "For one brief week I tasted the fullness of existence. But how to keep it going? That's what concerns me."

"Well, such an experience is actually an initiation into something else. I suspect this challenge has given you not only the self-esteem you were lacking but also the need to continue pushing the limits, uncovering new horizons, literally and figuratively. Surely now you must have more material for those essays you are writing."

172

"My perspective was altered by the foreign and natural beauty, that's for sure, and I did come to realize that life works best when there is a flow between times of intentional quiet and informed action."

"There you go. That's a beginning. Action needs a counterpoint and destiny always develops in silence. I think you've got it. By George, you've got it," she says, gently singing praises with a new skip in her step.

"Well, I suppose I am clear now about the ache."

"The what?"

"You know, the longing you feel when you need to find a new point of departure—when you need to shake your life up in order to find new intentions."

"Oh yes, we call that generativity."

"Well, whatever. This making and unmaking of myself has been germinating for some time now. I have learned more than I ever thought I would. I think everyone at my stage has to depart from the path of least resistance and set out on a new course. And if it involves a physical challenge, so much the better."

"Now you're talking," Joan says. " 'Please let your sun— your concentrated energy, your own submerged authentic vital power—shine out from you.' "

"Huh? A perfect sentiment. That is exactly what I'm talking about."

"A Japanese scholar, Raicho Hiratsuka, said that. In order not to fail in the end, you have to be dependent on yourself, and know that you can handle things, and most importantly, bring a little humor into the despair. Lightness, imagination, flexibility—these are the things that go into making a new start."

CHAPTER THIRTEEN

TAKING STAGE

It seems I'm a bit of a curiosity in this town. I wouldn't have realized it if Harriet, the librarian, hadn't called me a few weeks back to say that I had become the object of fascination. "First you run away from home and live like a hermit, and the next thing we hear, you are hiking the Inca Trail. We've had several requests for you to talk—mostly about Machu Picchu, but I'm sure no one would mind hearing about your year alone either. Few women do something that drastic," she continued. "We're curious as to what you learned in both situations."

"Actually, I'm still trying to sort that out," I replied. "I'm not sure I have much to offer, but making a speech might force some answers."

"How about late next month, say Saturday the thirtieth?" she asked.

"My calendar is wide open," I replied.

"It's a date then. I've got plenty of time to put it in the newsletter," she said, and we hung up. I felt an immediate surge of energy. Maybe a deadline looming would help me get something formulated that could go into print. Ever since Machu Picchu my thoughts and goals had started to gel, as had my writing. I couldn't wait to call Joan and tell her what had transpired.

"Hey, guess what?" I said, sounding breathless. "I've been asked to give a talk at the library. What do you think?"

"That's wonderful, dear. I knew it was only a matter of time. I told you that you were to be a people changer. You've already changed me."

"Oh, c'mon, that couldn't be so."

"Sure! You've got me out walking the beaches in all kinds of weather, looking for metaphors, letting the air blow through some of my more rugged moments. Maybe you were meant to inspire people to push their limits."

Her vote of confidence was all I needed. I dove right into the journal I kept on the Inca Trail and was dumbstruck by the uncensored voice that came alive in Peru:

Greeted by the thinning mists of dawn, the air comes into my tent with lemon blossom fingers to touch my sleepy face. Always there is the magical presence of nature. Before I even peek my head out into this tranquil world, I make sure to give thanks to the universe for

light, the Incas for the path, the elements for their
power, and the sun for its warmth, after which I crawl
out of the tent and stroll to a nearby stream to collect
water. My usual haste is slowed by the need to purify
the water, after which I set up my little one-burner stove
and wait for the coffee to perk. There is nothing better
than sipping hot coffee while sitting on a log between
towering cliffs and the music of rushing waters. Such is
my morning ritual. I take several deep breaths before
contemplating the day's itinerary. According to
Gustalvo, we are to climb up the ladder of the earth,
through barbed jungle thickets, then out of the steaming
forests into the open air and past small temples of
steeped stone....

How was I to share all this? I remembered Joan's suggestion that I play the role of reporter, and so I began to
ask myself the tough questions. For starters, why did I take
this challenge in the first place? I wasn't after the physical
experience—that's something I'd always shirked. Was it
my cousin's dare? I supposed so, and the fact that I had
been quietly envious of my grown kids who had hiked
both the Andes and the Himalayas—two adventures I'd
never dreamed were possible for me. It seemed a chance to
recapture my lost youth. I was eager to be reckless as well

as test my limits. Perhaps the trek was to prove to myself and my family that I wasn't nearly finished, only just getting going!

Then there was Joan's constant reminder never to refuse a call that would get me out of my head and into my body. Such a trek ensured that for once I took my body seriously, and while on the trail itself I was bound to be in touch with the elements. Joan believes there's no substitute for nature—without it you are doomed to a dull, lifeless existence. During my year alone, I came to depend on nature's lessons. And in exotic Peru the messages were all the more profound.

Walking the Inca Trail was much more of a spiritual quest than anything else. My outer world had shifted and I needed to find out who, in my aloneness, I was capable of being—how far I could go, stretch, and reach. The more I probed my memory and my notes, the more I began to make sense of the journey and why I had chosen to take it. This little talk would not sound like a travelogue or the tales of someone's overseas adventure. I was beginning to anticipate my minuscule debut with relish.

But with the appointed day at hand I am suddenly filled with the same trepidation that I felt when I started the

trek. It's just my ego, I tell myself, always wanting to per-
form in a way that people will like me. I soothe my jitters
by reminding myself that I have plenty of notes and lots of
pictures in case my memory fails me. Even so, I'm startled
as I pull into the parking lot and find it full. They couldn't
be here for me, could they? While in Peru I had committed to memory several sayings to bolster my courage, and
just now one, by the Native American Regal Black Swan,
comes to mind: "The only way to pass the test is to take
the test." Whether I'm giving a speech, walking my talk, or
climbing the mountain, it's all about taking one step and
then another. I lift my chin, walk toward the library door,
and head for the auditorium.

Much to my chagrin, the room is full—all ages and stages;
there are even a few men scattered among the crowd.
Obviously the idea of living alone or having wild adventures is more titillating than I thought. I swallow my nerves
and slink into the back row hoping to hide out before the
speech.

I can barely recall Harriet's introduction of me . . .
something about being a female Thoreau who was seeking
solace and suggestions for life from this fragile landscape
of Cape Cod as well as faraway Peru. Her description of
my odyssey sounds accurate enough, I think, while heading for the podium. I place my note cards in front of me

and take a moment to gaze at the crowd and make eye contact with Joan, who has positioned herself in the center of the room. She smiles warmly and then nods her head, as if to say, get on with it.

"I suppose the reason why I ran away from home in the first place was the need to depart from the prescribed path—to challenge myself like never before," I begin, already ignoring the speech I had prepared. "I had spent a lifetime playing the expected roles and being appropriate. Then one day, I simply decided it was time to exit the mainstream.

"My trip to Peru began with a similar desire to see if I could push my limits. Although I am no Everest-type mountain climber and hardly athletic, I had developed a yen for the unconventional and was craving departure from the safety of my existence. Having left many parts of my soul along the road over the course of a lifetime, I figured that such a trek might provide me with the chance to reclaim some of me. After all, according to the psychologist M. Scott Peck, "A life of wisdom must include contemplation, combined with action."

I pause for a moment and look around. There are no yawns, sleepy eyes, nodding heads—just eyes riveted on me. I take a breath, smile, and without looking back at my note cards, continue with my story.

"I came to realize that there are only 8,700 hours in a year and it is essential to make sure some of those hours are just for me. I was no longer waiting for my ship to come in—rather, I was swimming out to it, relishing each day rather than waiting for the future to take hold.

"It's all about being lost enough to want to find yourself," I tell the audience. "That isn't my line. Robert Frost said it, but it certainly defined me to a T. Being alone on Cape Cod during four seasons taught me the importance of retreat. Only if you take yourself away can you begin to repair and then regenerate." I look directly at Joan—knowing that I had hit one of her themes by mentioning a derivative of generativity: giving back, making something out of nothing, passing on what you know. She had told me that my strength was compassion. "You must have play-acted a lot as a child," she said, "because I've noticed that you always take on the concerns of the other person. You seem to have a tenderness for unappreciated people, as well. In order to help them, you've learned that you must understand where they are coming from."

While focusing on Joan, I lose my train of thought and glance at my notes for the first time. The entire speech has been a major digression, I realize. But from the reaction of my listeners, which includes laughter, tears, and much nodding of heads, I feel as though I must have touched a chord. In any case, no one has gotten up to leave, and many are still on the edge of their chairs. I glance at the clock on the back wall. One hour has elapsed. Surely it's time to draw my comments to a close. "And so," I say, "I wish for all of you that you remain as unfinished as the shoreline along the beach and that you continue to transcend yourselves again and again."

The applause is deafening. As I gather my note cards, eager to proceed to my chair, the librarian asks if I would be willing to answer a few questions, after which several hands go up. I call on a slightly graying woman in the second row who wants to know why I left my husband out of both my journeys. "Are we meant to travel alone?" she asks.

"I don't honestly know how we can find our true selves in the midst of the crowd," I answer. "I think retreating alone is the only way to understand what needs repair. The isolation forces you to ask the questions we all seem to want to avoid. So yes, we all must go it alone at some point. There is no alternative."

Still the question persists. "Can you get the same result, closer to home?" a thirty-something woman asks. "Must such journeys always be exotic?"

"Well, Cape Cod was pretty close to me," I surmise.

"This familiar and simple place got me started. With no plan or agenda—no achievable goals in sight—I let my life happen for a change. Then that mountain air in Peru offered clarity for future paths. It didn't have to be Peru. But I had to go someplace distinctly different."

"What was so miserable in your life anyway that made you run away?" a man in the front row asks. I hesitate, stumped by his question. My cheeks become beet red. What had been so wrong? And how much am I obliged to tell this perfect stranger? I swallow and proceed, figuring I have to spit out the truth.

"My marriage was stale, for starters. There had been several deaths in the family, and my career as a children's book author seemed to be dwindling. But when it comes right down to it, I really couldn't figure out how to grow and change without taking leave from the familiar."

"Sounds awfully self-serving," he continues. "Would you call yourself a feminist?"

"Not really," I respond quickly, feeling a bit angry at his assumption. "I've always despised any word that ends in *ist*. Communist, Marxist, terrorist . . . they all seem angry and harsh. I suppose if I were to label me at this point I would call myself a proponent of feminine energy. You know this world we live in has been designed almost totally by men. Not that I have anything against men, but our institutions are sort of out of balance—wouldn't you say?" He doesn't react, but many of the others begin to nod. "For my part, I was working hard, staying too much in my head and becoming 'manly' in the process. Something was missing. I have come to believe that what had evaporated from me was my soft, intuitive, instinctive side. That's what I was in search of, really, and I believe I found her again."

The audience responds—clapping, nodding, and beaming. I'd best quit while I'm ahead, I think, and then one more hand pops up.

"Was the trek to test your physical prowess or emotional endurance?" a stunning woman, dressed in running clothes, asks.

"I should say both. It was indeed dramatic, arriving at the Sun Gate, knowing I had achieved the goal of finishing, but at that point it wasn't a feeling of winning or losing something. Rather it was about the unique experience of a newfound kinship with myself and finally feeling that my body, soul, and spirit were all connected."

Harriet, who has been standing nearby, mercifully moves toward the podium before another question can be asked, thus bringing the session to a close. As I gather up my things, several people surround the podium, bringing with them lingering thoughts or private queries. Out of the corner of my eye I see that Joan is taking it all in. It is her reaction to this afternoon's performance that I seek the most. As the crowd thins, she waves from the back of the room and comes forward. "It's time, my dear. We'd best be going," she says, giving me an excuse to depart from the crowd.

"Your house or mine?" I ask.

"I think we should take a walk on the beach," she suggests. "It's a beautiful day and we do our best talking down there, wouldn't you say?"

Once there, we waste no time taking off our sandals and rolling up our slacks. I take hold of Joan's arm and we head down the boardwalk toward the shore. The surf is frothy, with whitecaps rolling in from as far as I can see—a jubilant sea, complementing the high energy I possess at the moment. "So, what did you think?" I ask eagerly.

"People are impressed to hear about someone taking time in this impatient age, exploring the territory of being, no less." I catch myself smiling broadly. "You have something unique to share, my dear. People are dying for adventure, and if they can't make themselves get out there, they will content themselves with living vicariously off of others."

"What sorts of things did I actually say? It's sounds silly, but it's already a blur."

"You touched on all the important points—the need for independence, the importance of solitude, the desire to find your personhood again, staying present, engaging your senses, aligning thoughts and feelings with your body."

"I said all that? Good. Then I truly have begun to absorb the lessons."

"What lessons?"

"Yours," I say impishly. "It was you who made me new, or at least you pushed me toward the brink."

"Goody," she says, though I think she is thrilled not so much by the compliment as by my evolution.

My feet are in the water now—the surf splashing my calves and dampening my clothes. Finally I can unwind and simply digest the experience.

"I particularly liked your phrase 'the second journey.' Those insights are intriguing, dear. I never gave my departures a label as such, but the term certainly harnesses the ideal. It's true. We must literally be willing to begin again and again over the course of a lifetime. You really can't know what it is you are supposed to do unless you depart from the mundane and refire your spirit. That's the way to generativity. I'm so glad you were able to conceptualize it and put the idea out there."

"I can't take credit for the term *second journey*," I tell her. "It is the title of a book. But ever since reading it some years ago, I have harbored the desire to develop a self beyond all the roles I play, wanting more than ever to know the reason for my own personal life and then doing something with my newfound insights."

"Well, I suspect a combination of living alone, probing your psyche, and then taking off for the magic of Machu Picchu has made you a little odd—but in a good way, of course. I think you have gotten yourself a vocation."

"A what?"

"A summons of sorts—something you are responding to. I think you are meant to guide people back to themselves—get them out of the mold. The great loneliness is that most people don't know who they are."

I find myself thinking that success certainly feels better than distress. "Perhaps I can finally start writing these thoughts which are just now coming together for me. The momentum is certainly there."

"But remember, dear, you don't have to tell all. I got a little uncomfortable when that man started pushing you to talk about why you ran away. You didn't have to give him everything you had."

"I was only trying to make myself credible."

"You did that early on, with your sincerity and vitality. Telling too much can be titillating as well as charming, but a little goes a long way. Remember, secrets are power. Strangers don't deserve to know the intimate side of your life. It's none of their damn business. I adore all your wild and salty ways, but we've become friends and we need truth to pass between us. The rest of you, the public person, needs to censor what you tell and show."

"Boundaries are not my forte, you know."

"I know, but don't forget how I was portrayed in that little local newspaper story a few months back. That reporter, unbeknownst to me, was inspecting my dress, manner, house, and words as if she had me under a microscope. That will be happening to you. As I see it, you are to become a cheerleader, urging others on with your enthusiasm. They are not to take your specific path—they are meant to find their own way. You are simply providing the incentive or challenge."

We have reached the end of the beach and stand at the base of the jetty—the very place where we met several years before. How was I to know that she would dare me to be different, and in doing so, I would reinvent my life. It occurs to me that I have loosened up—that living on the edge has made me eminently responsive, so much so that I could hear the call. Suddenly, everything is converging and I am being lifted to the next level of progress.

"I am no longer in the fog," I say to her.

"Nor am I," she answers, taking my hand and leading me back along the shore.

CHAPTER FOURTEEN

SWAN SONG

M y creative energies soared after the speech. I had found a voice, or at least believed that I had a voice and, more important, some ideas worth sharing with other people. What's more, a slew of metaphors and simi-les were popping into my mind with little or no effort as I scoured the dunes and retraced my steps.

Joan, too, was on a roll. The formation of the ninth stage was becoming so clear to her that she could hardly contain herself, calling me frequently to read a perfected line or a newly revised clever paragraph. It was with such fervor that she sent off a letter to her editor at Norton, alerting him to the fact that she was developing something important.

But alas, one month went by and then another and she didn't hear a word. She was quietly annoyed, but fortu-nately she didn't share my fear that time had passed her by— that the respect accorded her when Erik was alive had evaporated after his passing. There is a lot of prejudice in this culture where elders are concerned, and I couldn't help but imagine that the people at her publishing house pictured her sitting in a rocking chair with time on her hands, lacking all motivation. For once I kept my feelings to myself.

And then one day while we were having lunch, her editor called, his interest piqued, and Joan became as animated as I have ever seen her.

"In two weeks?" she said, quickly grabbing her date book. "That would be fine. Yes, Wednesday sounds good. Eleven-thirty? That's perfectly doable. Until then," and with that she hung up.

"So, will you take me?" she asked, planting a direct gaze on me. "I'm not beyond taking a little trip to New York. How about it? I think it's the only way to get the job done." And then she sweetened the proposal. "Besides, I've been wanting to introduce you to my editor. You could be my additional excuse."

She no sooner had my agreement than she went directly to her bedroom closet. Like any woman determined to make an impression, her next move was to find her favorite jacket, around which she would design her ensemble. Then she turned her gaze on me.

It wasn't enough that I should be driving her; I, too, had to present myself well. "This is your publishing debut," she informed me. "You'd best look the part."

"I thought I was just going along for the ride."

"Oh, no. You're going to need a publisher one of these days. Here's your chance. You've done the inward work, but now you need to show, in your outward appearance, how secure you've become. It's all about integration, dear. The outfit you wore for your library speech didn't begin to reflect your true nature, nor show off your body. You seem to be hiding behind drapy clothes and long hair."

"Really," I said, mildly offended, although I suspected she was dead right.

"You don't represent yourself. You're in the people business. It's time to look more mature and show that you have a high regard for what you do."

"But that's just it—what do I do? I don't exactly have a real career yet."

"You're an author, that's what you are. Just because you are shifting genres doesn't take away from the fact that you've been writing all kinds of stories for some twenty years now. I'd consider that job description enough for an author."

It was good to hear someone respect the work I do. Up until recently I've been grinding out material simply as a bearable way to make a living. But Joan seemed to have higher aspirations for me and that was intriguing.

"Whenever I appear anywhere," she continued with

her pitch, "I'm careful to represent who I am, and you've got to begin to do the same. I want them to take you seriously in New York."

The very idea was certainly appealing, but my mind always draws a blank when it comes to style. Fretting about clothes and hair seemed like something best left back in adolescence.

"Either people pay no attention to their clothing and risk being misunderstood or they pay too much and risk being disingenuous. I'm not suggesting that you need a façade. It's just that a total stranger needs to get it the minute you walk over his or her threshold. Your work, your intentions, your goals all become evident when the total package is just right. Understand?"

Not really, but I nod affirmatively anyway.

"You want your individuality to shine," she said as I find myself observing her as never before. Her style matches the elegant bareness of her home—sleek, stark, yet warm because of all the earthen tones in the furniture and wall coloring. That day she was dressed in black slacks and a black sweater over which she wore a tunic-length quilted vest in mauve and gray. She finished her look with chunky beads made of natural stones that she had collected on the Oregon shore. My old blue woolen skirt and faded top suddenly felt dowdy and very uncreative.

"I adopted my look at Harvard," she continued, "right after attending my first faculty wives meeting. There I was in a roomful of women dressed in tweed suits with bouffant hairdos, and I was in shock. Where was the individuality? Would I be expected to conform as well? I walked away from that experience saying no way, not me, and headed straight for a store which sold exotic and colorful clothes from India, buying several pairs of leotards to wear under unusual jackets and smocks."

"But you knew what satisfied you, what was comfortable."

"Come along. We'll rummage through my things," she said, ushering me upstairs toward her cedar closet. There, hanging neatly, was a color-coordinated array of jersey skirts, pants, and handsome jackets, most of which looked as if they had been handcrafted. "You need to pick out something based on the qualities that you, as a writer and speaker, want to emphasize. Here, try this on for size," she suggested, pulling out a brown, beige, rust, and black patchwork jacket that would look terrific with my blond hair.

"I have a jersey dress that might be perfect underneath," I said, turning toward the mirror, pleased with what I saw.

"Here's another, more colorful vest. An artist friend of mine designed it."

"They're both stunning."

"Well, take them home and think about it. We can't rush these decisions. It's important that you feel you've found your own costume, not just accept what someone else thinks might work well for you."

Just yesterday we were playing dress-up, and now I feel a vague sense of destiny as we barrel south on Route 95 heading for New York City and the offices of W. W. Norton. It was decided that we should leave around five A.M. to give us plenty of time to get to the city for a luncheon meeting. All was in place. Our jackets on hangers swaying to and fro in the back, her neatly typed manuscript, boxed and sitting on the seat, a change of clothes and our nightwear stuffed into a canvas bag in case we had to stay the night, and a cooler with snacks. "We've missed the rush hours in both Providence and New Haven," I tell Joan, who has just emerged from a catnap. "Barring anything unforeseen, we should be in the city with plenty of time to freshen up."

"Quite a shock to see all these big buildings, isn't it, dear?" Joan says as we pass through Stamford and approach the city. "Quite a change from our little town, isn't it?"

"You're not getting cold feet now, are you?" I ask.

"Hell, no. I can hardly wait. If anything, uncertainty makes me sizzle. When you've done your homework, and I sure have, it's all fun after that. Besides when something is important to me, I can be gutsy and stand my ground."

I recall something Henry Miller wrote: "The heroine enjoys her life by rearranging it according to her needs. She may say she is doing it for others, for humanity, but we know that she lies . . . the heroine knows that right here is where things happen, not somewhere else . . . that the world for her is a place where things are engendered and brought to life."

"Do you have a plan or agenda?" I ask.

"Not really. Just making an appearance should be a statement in and of itself, don't you think? And after that, keep it light. I'm not desperate; I have the past to lean on, after all. There is strength in that, my dear, as well as confidence. Besides, I am almost certain that I've gotten the ninth stage right," she says, sounding invincible.

"These sorts of meetings scare the daylights out of me. I've never been good at selling myself or my ideas."

"Don knows that Erik and I were always a collaboration. I would think that he is expecting to find much of Erik in this, my latest work. In any case, I'm simply sharing what I've concluded. This experience is not about selling, it's about persuasion, which needs to be playful from beginning to end. It's a game. There are rules, but there must always be play."

"Friendly persuasion."

"Hey, I like that. I will introduce my ideas in an artful way. I think he's going to love the idea that transcendence is really about transcen*dance*! Anyhow, the minute the discussion smacks of teaching or preaching, I know I've lost."

We are on the East River Drive with time to spare. I pull off at the Seventy-ninth Street exit and into the first available garage, anxious to dump the car and the pressures that come with driving in the city. It is only after we hail a cab that I realize we don't have Norton's address.

"No problem," Joan assures me. "Take us to the New York Public Library," she tells the driver, "the one at Forty-second Street." Then she turns to me. "Norton's right across the street." She smiles, ever so sure of herself.

"How many times have you done this, anyway?" I ask, utterly baffled by her assurance.

"Too many to count." She sits back as her eyes drink in the varied sights and sounds that only a city like New York offers. "I feel so awake," she bubbles. "Thank goodness I'm still up to it."

We grab hold of the ceiling grips above our windows as the driver winds in and out of the traffic, hitting a few potholes in the process. "I hadn't planned on going to an amusement park," she giggles as we dodge pedestrians and buses. She is craning her neck to locate her building as we stop in front of the library. Once out into the street, Joan points her cane. "This way," she announces, without hesitation.

I always find the cacophony of New York traffic disconcerting, and today, as I hold on to the arm of a somewhat fragile old woman, I am perplexed as to how to navigate us across the street. One taxi has just slammed into another, generating a chorus of honking horns. To make matters worse, a delivery truck is blocking the entire left lane and an ambulance is trying to edge its way forward. Joan, oblivious to all the commotion, simply raises her cane and leads us from one curb to another. Sure enough the traffic halts, just as if she were Moses parting the Red Sea. "That's never happened before," she says, mildly delighted with herself. "I guess there's some worth to aging. But I must admit, New York is not a good place for old people. It feels like we're just in the way."

"Here we are," she announces triumphantly as we approach Norton's front door. She pauses for a second, pulls herself up straight, and reaches for the large brass door handle. Once inside, she heads straight for the elevator and in minutes we alight at the appropriate floor and make our way toward the receptionist. I glance into a nearby mirror, adjust my jacket, and fluff up my shortened hair. "Hello, Mrs. Erikson," the receptionist says, before Joan has a chance to announce herself. "Mr. Lamm is expecting you."

I trail behind as she heads down the hall passing an assortment of editors and secretaries, all of whom greet her by name. Not only has she arrived at old age knowing just how to respond to life, but she has arrived back in New York City with the confidence of a thirty-year-old. We wind around several corridors until finally we are at the end of the line where, tucked in a corner, is the spacious office of Norton's publisher. I stand back as the performance begins.

"Well, hello there, Joan. Come in, come in. It's so good to see you again," Don Lamm says, rushing across his office. "And how do you do?" he says, surely wondering who I am.

"Joan Anderson," I say, extending my hand. "I'm the chauffeur," I offer, not having thought how I might characterize myself.

"More than that," Joan chimes in. "She's my friend and confidante," Joan gushes, "and a writer in her own right," she adds, thus getting in her intended plug.

Alas, it is obvious this is Joan's day, not mine, as Mr.

Lamm motions her toward the brown leather chair directly across from his desk. I note her hesitation after she settles in as she peruses the setting and reestablishes her equilibrium. "How was the trip? Did you come in last night?" he asks, breaking up the awkward pause.

"Nope," Joan answers. "We left early this morning. Returning later today, as well. I'm retired, you know," she says with a twinkle.

"It doesn't seem so to me," he continues, eyeing the box that I am clutching. I was about to hand it over and then remember that when Joan is holding court, she controls the day. "So, what have you come up with in terms of the stages?" he probes. "I've been trying to guess where your ideas were taking you ever since our phone conversation."

"Well, it's been quite a process," she begins, warming up to the moment. "I used to think that when you got to be old you plateaued somehow. But I've come to see how we are all capable of learning new tricks. As long as we are alive, we must keep transforming ourselves," she says with confidence.

I can't hide my grin. Isn't she doing just that by her very presence here today?

"It's rather curious, but no matter how old we are, we're always troubled by inexperience—always searching for direction. Don't you agree?"

He nods, utterly delighted with her as she rattles off her most innovative ideas.

"Wake up! Stay awake! I say. You know, faith and hope, those strengths we gained when we were young, are all the more important in old age. Pity that we use such small amounts of any of our strengths through the stages," she continues, and then turns to me. "Why don't you pass the box along to Don."

He raises the top gently and then lifts the crisp white pages out of the box. I imagine that he expected less—certainly not the substantial pile of pages that are now in front of him.

"So you say we can still maintain some semblance of autonomy and growth in old age?" he asks her.

"Indeed. But only if we've taken care of our bodies," she responds, straightening up in a most beguiling way. "The consistent care necessary to keep the body machinery functioning in spite of age and deterioration is mandatory. A lifetime of training is required. It's so easy to blame the terrain, so to speak, or the light and wind for our failures and backsliding. But where the body is concerned there is no time for self-pity."

"Come to think of it, it seems obvious and yet, I've never seen such a concept in print," he concurs.

"It's no wonder, living as we do in a society that wants

to put old people to bed. You can hardly get wisdom out of someone who is lying around during his last years. Actuality is needed right up until the end. Does that make sense?"

"It certainly does," he says, turning over one page, then another, stopping to read a few lines, then flipping over the paper, all the while listening with one ear. "That's why I felt it was so important for you to continue Erik's work. And from the looks of things, it appears as though you have."

"Well, I hope so. I consider myself one of the fortunate ones. After all, I have a platform—a chance to speak and be heard. Some of my friends aren't so lucky." Already, Joan has made him look beyond her frail and aging body to her mind, which seems sharper than ever just now.

"I love it when I get to the essence of something," she says, continuing to present her newfound point of view. "But I came upon a real stumbling block writing the ninth stage. No matter how you look at it, old age is more negative than positive. The negative pulls are greater and therefore an aging person has to strive that much harder to gain strength. I was stumped for a time in the writing because I didn't want to admit to myself, perhaps, how difficult this last stage was—more difficult than any of the others."

"I'll be eager to read your conclusions," Mr. Lamm says,

flipping ahead to get a glimpse of what's to come. From the interest in his eyes, it seems that Joan has delivered a product her publisher wants. "Well," he says, satisfied that a publishable document is in his hands, "how about some lunch? I've made a reservation at the Yale Club."

"Lovely," Joan agrees.

I am utterly appalled that instead of hailing a cab he takes hold of Joan's arm and we proceed to walk the several blocks to the restaurant, making small talk all the way. No problem for Joan, who seems to be thriving on the city's sensations. Steadied by her cane, she matches him step for step, and we are sitting down at a window table in the club in no time. Business accomplished, with everyone in a celebratory mood, they converse about recent history or memories of other deals long ago.

"How have you gotten on since Erik's passing?" he asks.

"Well, one can't stay in the muck forever now, can one? Erik and I had talked so often about living way beyond what we wrote," she says, taking a bite of her turkey club. "Anyway, I was well aware of what he would have wanted to write. I suppose it was a way of staying connected with him, if you know what I mean."

"But how did you manage the mechanics of it?" he asks.

"Well, I have a lot of support on the Cape," she continues, giving a nod to me. "My friend here had been goading me for months, and then my old secretary moved in to make the process move along more efficiently. I'm not done yet," she announces, surprising even me. "There's a journal of Erik's I need to translate and, after that, some of my poetry."

The wine continues to flow, as do shared memories of past projects and gossip about mutual friends, until the lunch hour is long past. "If we hope to beat the rush hour," I interject, "we'd best be going."

We hail a cab and sink into the backseat, our adrenaline highs now beginning to deflate. "I always need to try on new capacities," she says as she leans her head back against the headrest, reliving her soul-satisfying day. "Although I would have preferred visiting Norton with Erik, today it feels gratifying to have succeeded solo. Life is a response, isn't it, dear?" she says, her voice far away for the moment as we head toward the parking garage.

"Indeed. And you certainly did a great job of responding today! What amazes me, Joanie, is that the more hurdles you are presented with, the more energetic you become in an effort to leap over them. You're a veritable racehorse, for heaven's sake. I feel like you just won the Kentucky Derby."

"Really, dear. How lovely," she says, pleased with the

compliment, especially in light of the adversity elders face in the ninth stage of life—things like weakened strength, the threat of nursing homes, being removed from the community—all issues and situations she has managed to avoid.

I sit beside a victor. She came, she saw, and she surely conquered. Her words were valued as were her ideas and ideals. Having sensed the grander picture and looked beyond her limits, she is more than surviving now. She is thriving.

We depart the city, road weary but sated, nonetheless, having had the most triumphant of days.

CHAPTER FIFTEEN

LIFE CYCLE COMPLETED

By her own admission Joan has grown shabby and old. Her body is beginning to present problems: her once broken hip is faltering, her heart is growing faint, and, worst of all, her short-term memory is the cause of frequent confusion. A combination of events finally have forced a move to an assisted living facility on the outskirts of town. Although her accommodations include a large studio apartment at the end of the hall with a sweeping view of lawn and forest behind, losing her autonomy and the ability to control her personal time has taken its toll.

Still, she is familiar with the institutional routine, having been in several such facilities for rehab, not to mention Erik's lengthy stay. She has learned to make them work for her, especially by getting extra time in their training rooms. "It's a matter of testing your capacities and preparing for the next level, dear. Old age demands that we garner and lean on all previous experience. I will never forget how I started out as a lonely child with little else but a body to depend on. Having practiced my whole life to be independent, I have these virtues to lean on now."

Today is her ninety-fourth birthday, and she is her
most feisty self. A party has been planned, and she will
push aside any regrets about having to leave her home in
favor of the glee she is sure to feel with the gathering of
so many friends.

As I approach the parlor, the din tells me this is no
small crowd, nor is it a group of old ladies. Once beyond
the French doors, I find a variety of people—Harvard professors, young families, artists, doctors, gerontologists,
family members. I recognize only a few people—those who
have stopped by to visit her recently—so I'm quite happy
to retreat to a comfortable corner and attempt to untangle
the threads of people and ideas intertwined with hers, celebrating not just a birthday but their connectedness.

Never have I witnessed such a collective moment. It is
obvious they are like-minded souls, most of whom have
been marked or altered by Joan in some way, and everyone
is wishing to draw more nourishment from her naughty
twinkle, upbeat intonation, and playfulness. Although her
life is spinning out its thread, she appears as if she is celebrating the midway mark—dressed down in a purple T-
shirt advertising a 12K run, black vest and black pants, no
jewelry but with a smile that widens with the arrival of

each new guest. She continues to prove that old age comes gently to those who have made their own rules and followed their lessons.

"It's you!" she says to one well-wisher, making him feel as if he were the only person at the party. "However did you get here? Fresh off the book tour, aye? Isn't this fun? Make sure you talk with Richard. You seem to be researching the same topic. Can you stay afterward? Perhaps we can really get into things then. Oh, what a great day. Aren't birthdays wonderful?"

She's off and running to one person after another in her most receiving of moods, aiming for the whole, forgoing inhibition. "You must be willing to be receptive," she told me once. "Otherwise you ruin the gift."

"I feel light as a feather," I overhear her proclaim. "This place is busting with action. We should have more parties or circuses, for that matter, if for no other reason than to have yet another excuse to play, don't you think?"

As she laughs at her own joke a young woman appears in the doorway carrying a bouquet of balloons. "For me?" Joan shouts, sweeping across the room, arms outstretched. "My favorite thing," she says, taking hold of the ribbons and twirling around, looking very much like a happy clown, before handing a purple balloon to a small child nearby and an orange one to his sibling.

I am entranced by this scene. There she stands, buoyed by a handful of balloons, a colorful woman in her nineties—nothing black and white about Joan. I'm amused that not one balloon is pink, the color she detests because she was made to wear it throughout her childhood, while her older sister got the coveted blue. No wonder that when she wove the stages she chose mostly primary colors. And just then I understand my fascination with this picture. Whether intended or not, she holds eight balloons, one for each color of the eight stages. As amazed as I am to see this coincidence, I am more in awe that Joan continues to demonstrate the truth and vitality of her hard-earned strengths—hope, will, purpose, competence, love, generativity, and, of course, wisdom. With all these people around vying for a moment of her attention, I find myself thinking that she got somewhat stuck in generativity—so eager to pass on her zest for life, knowing full well how a teacher's influence never stops.

"I'm so glad so many of you were in need of play today," she says, passing off the balloons as a waitress offers a cup of tea. After plunking in two cubes of sugar, she begins stirring it, not looking up but continuing a conversation with a bearded, bespectacled gentleman who has obviously asked her about the last two stages, his attention rapt.

"There are losses," she says. "Our bodies wear out, our thoughts come more slowly. But our life cycles are our most creative effort. We can't ever not be in them, right? The struggle is to try and obtain a sense of participation in your life the whole way through. We must treasure old age," she continues, "but not wallow in nostalgia. Appreciate the joy of attachment without the possessiveness."

"You're an original, Joan," he says, shaking his head in both amazement and agreement.

"Not really," she answers, in a full and reassuring voice. "Looking around at some of my older friends, I see that their lives appear rather uneventful on the surface. Yet most of them, when put to the test, know what really matters. Everyone has kernels of wisdom and original thoughts buried inside, don't you think? Deep within every life, no matter how dull or ineffectual, something eternal is happening."

"I couldn't agree more," the gentleman says. "It's just that some people, like yourself, find a forum, while others do not."

"You're right, there. And what's worse, people tend to take advantage of old age. You have to be a strong old person. When I went to see my editor recently, I was intentionally making a statement. I've learned to lean on my past and what I've done when I need to make the necessary impression."

Several others have gathered around as she continues to improvise. Why didn't someone arrange for a band? I think. We should all be dancing! And yet she is dancing without music—dancing with her eyes, and her gestures, unable to be still, enlivened as she is by all the fuss. She moves as if at a ball, all the while popping tea sandwiches into her mouth and then pausing occasionally to accumulate her sense of it all. "Give me a little ecstasy," she has asked of me from time to time.

"What's that?" I would ask.

"It's just the excitement of beauty, really. It's not to be forced. It's a process, not a goal. Joy can be a goal, but ecstasy can't. It happens when you get to the point where everything is perfectly satisfactory, the way you wanted it to be, when you can't get it any better, when you are just there, hit the nail on the head. It's a wonderful thing." Someone clinks a glass and the chatter stops—rapt attention now, all eyes on the woman of the hour. Joan looks around like an expectant child, living in the openness to the wonder of being alive, no matter how much longer.

This crowd knows what pleases her—not things, but

qualities such as touch, a kiss, or kind words. Someone has written a poem about hope, play, and how she delights in every day, followed by a song, the cake, and numerous toasts. As her eyes glisten, she glances around the room, making contact with each singing voice, cementing the memory. "You've got to remember everything," she would counsel me, "the highs and the lows. Don't let them go into the scrap basket just because the moment is over. These are the treasures that you wear for the rest of time. They are meant to be around your neck. As you fondle each pearl, you can say to yourself, ah yes, I remember."

"Ms. Anderson. Ms. Anderson," a voice whispers. I am startled out of my stupor and turn to see who's there. "Visiting hours are over," the nurse says, standing nearby with medications in her hand.

"Of course," I answer, having all but forgotten just where I was. I shake my head and glance at the clock on the wall—three hours have passed.

"It's hard, I know," she says, her gentle sympathy a welcome comfort. "Obviously she meant a lot to you," she adds. I'm stung by her referring to Joan as if she is already gone. Still, she hasn't moved a muscle the entire time I have been sitting here. Nevertheless I am still finding this scene hard to fathom because there have been so many times that I have gone to her house and found her still and asleep—in repose, looking far away. But each time she has awakened. A chilling feeling surrounds my heart.

"You have brought me so far," I whisper. "Can you hear my gratitude?" Lost in my pain, I fail to see her stirrings or notice that her eyes have opened. Her long graceful arms reach upward as she pulls me toward her chest. Always the gatherer right up to the end. We are breathing together, her faint heartbeat still recognizable and then gradually, her arms go limp and I am released.

I pick myself up and stand beside the bed for one last look. She wears an expression of contentment. "He who loved his life can love his death, as well," said Theodore Roethke, and so it seems to be. "Good-bye," I say, "Goodbye, my friend," and then I quickly take leave, daring not to dally, except at the nurse's station. "Do you expect her to last the night?" I ask.

"We never know," she answers, almost apologetically, and I move on, struck by the fact that no matter how technologically advanced we've become there is no digitizing these huge moments.

I walk out the door. The sultry night feels full of clo-

sure. Take action, even in the face of death, Joan would advise. My pace quickens as if walking fast and moving on to
the next event will numb this departing moment. I swallow hard while starting up the engine and back out, the
tires squealing in my haste as I pull onto the tiny two-lane
road. Coincidentally, Mozart's Requiem is being played on
the classical station, and I turn up the volume, counting on
the music to dull my pain. Where should I go? What
should I do? I can't just drive home and walk back into my
life as if nothing has happened.

Minutes later, I find myself in the parking lot of
the Pleasant Bay General Store. Slow down. Take time,
breathe, I tell myself. If I've learned nothing else from the
experiences of the past few years it is to know the empty
space that always accompanies change. There is no beginning without a thorough and satisfactory ending. I lean my
head back against the seat and then the tears well up.
"Joanie, Joanie, Joanie," I say in rhythm with my sobbing.
"Love is a wonderful thing but it hurts," she had said after
saying good-bye to one of her children. Still she loved her
emotions, all of them. "Lengthen the hug," she would tell
me, "hold the kiss, stop avoiding, look at what is happening. Give in to it, be it a good or bad experience, or you'll
miss it altogether."

Ten to fifteen minutes pass when a police car pulls up

alongside my car and flashes a light in the window. "Are you all right?" he asks.

I simply nod and then dab my eyes and nose with a tissue. "I'll be leaving soon," I say. "I just said good-bye to a good friend and I'm a little bit sad."

I seem to need to extend the night, perhaps as a way to extend her life. Passing by some of her haunts might cement the memories. I turn the ignition and continue toward town. Nothing in this place will ever be quite the same again. I'm drawn toward the church and gaze up at the steeple, normally lit in someone's memory but dark tonight. I must call the minister in the morning and have it lit for Joan. Give over to the spirit of the evening, I tell myself. A lifetime is burning in this moment—there is something very holy about this night.

I move on, driving no more than twenty miles per hour and am led to Parallel Street, where her little green-and-yellow clapboard house sits—darkened now, the shades drawn. A once lively abode now looking unkempt and forlorn—birdfeeders abandoned, Saint Christopher's statue nowhere in sight. A pile of newspapers in the driveway signal that the resident has been gone for sometime. Down the street a ways I pass her tiny bench, a frail-looking wooden-and-metal structure, not unlike how she appeared, yet a bench strong enough to handle most anybody, also the hallmark of Joan, who had been a comfort and inspiration to so many.

It is the night of a half moon—bright enough to dim the stars—the kind of evening that calls for meditation, nostalgia, remembered lines of poetry. I have had all that. In a sense, sitting by her bedside, I walked the beach with her one last time—covered our tracks, reviewed our positions, surfaced from the confusion, and now the high tide will once again erase any sign that we have been here. Still, it seems fitting to head for the beach one last time.

The sun has long since fallen into the sea, making the sky feel all the more huge and bright—brighter than ever tonight because of a glowing Mars. As a frothy high tide drowns out my thoughts, my energy rises and I am exhilarated once again by nothing more than the playful sea. I sink down on a darkened dune here on the very beach where Joan and I met. Isn't it funny how little accidental meetings turn out to be main features in one's life. It was just three weeks ago we sat on this very dune munching on tuna fish sandwiches, saying little but drinking in the scene. She had been fascinated by the antics of little children that day and how their parents delighted in them. "If this were your last day on earth," I happened to ask her, "what would be some of the things you would want to say?"

"Make time for play each day," she answered without giving the question a moment's thought. "We're asses if we don't. Nobody is going to force you to—no one says go out and play. It's a shame there is no philosophy of life anywhere that insists on play."

"Anything specific that you enjoy the most?" I continued.

"Look, there isn't anything that I do that I don't enjoy. If I do it then I enjoy it. But playful activities are the best because they are goalless, the result is unknown, and they are full of fantasy, imagination, and random discovery. What can beat that?"

Her voice is as clear in death as it was in life. What's more, her words are now pushing me beyond grief. I head for the shore, taking Joan's fierce spirit with me for one last walk. *"Spirit, spirit of gentleness, blow through the wilderness, calling and free,"* I begin singing, as it is one of Joan's favorite hymns—*"Spirit, spirit of restlessness, stir me from placidness, wind, wind on the sea."* Yes, yes, there is enchantment even in the passing because she is and remains a vital part of my tapestry.

"I really thought that when you got old you stopped

learning: I thought it was a plateau," she told me. "The fact that each day you learn something new never crossed my mind and that's fun! So, I advise you to take care of yourself and let yourself grow old."

She has delivered the charge. I pick up a moon shell and toss it into the sea. "May your journey continue," I say to her, with much gratitude for the launching of mine.

LIFE LINES

JOAN ERIKSON'S UNCONVENTIONAL WISDOM

OVERDOSE ON THE SENSES

"*Get out of your body, absorbing all that you come in contact with.*"

DANCE BEYOND THE BREAKERS

"*Having direction and going after something—going toward that which gives you purpose is the way—otherwise your life becomes avoiding trouble and there is no strength in that.*"

LEAN ON YOUR STRENGTHS

"*In order not to fail in the end, you have to be dependent on yourself and know that you can handle things. Most importantly, bring a little humor into despair. Lightness, imagination, flexibility—these are the things that go into making a new start.*"

SPONSOR YOURSELF

"*Don't deny yourself to please others. You only lose yourself in the promise.*"

SHARE WHAT YOU KNOW

"*Be generative. Pass on what you know. In sharing there is real delight. People in every stage depend on other people. Out of con-*

nection real growth happens. If there is no reciprocity, nothing ever works."

PLAY OUT YOUR EXPERIENCES

"We don't stop playing because we grow old. We grow old because we stop playing. Anyway, the opposite of play is obey!"

REACH FOR SATISFACTION

"Does what you are doing (in work or play) satisfy you? Does it make you laugh? Does it make you sing? If so, latch on to it."

ALWAYS BE WILLING TO EMBRACE CHALLENGES

"A good life is like a weaving. Energy is created in the tension. The struggle, the pull and tug are everything."

ACKNOWLEDGMENTS

Writing a book is a collaborative process. The encouragement, suggestions, and cooperation of many people made it possible to bring Joan Erikson's ideals into story form.

The seed for this book was planted by Bishop John Thornton. He insisted that "she was the story—that she had much to say" and that I should try to document her blithe spirit. Allison Humenuk, a documentary filmmaker, volunteered to capture Joan on film. This project was funded by many of Joan's friends from her days in Belvedere, California, particularly Dick and Zoila Schoenbrun, who had great enthusiasm for anything that had to do with Joan Erikson.

My mother, Joyce Anderson, was intrigued by Joan and had us both to tea many an afternoon. My husband, Robin, gave me space and time to create a manuscript worthy of the woman, as did my assistant, Debbie Ebersold. Even my grandson Carson said prayers at night when he knew I was blocked. My friend Pam Borman insisted from the beginning that "I sit at her feet—that she was a goddess of sorts and her message needed to be shared." And Marilyn Leugers participated in some of the weaving sessions, thus introducing another perspective to the process. The women who have attended my Weekends by the Sea have continually asked to know Joan more thoroughly. Such nudging from so many ensured that this book would come into being.

But this project would not have come to fruition without the suggestions and support of those in the literary world who know books: my agent, Olivia Blumer; my editors, Gerry Howard and Anne Merrow; and my publicist, Heather Maguire. To you four, I am both grateful and indebted.

JOAN ANDERSON is a seasoned journalist who has also written numerous children's novels, including *1787: The First Thanksgiving Feast* and *The American Family Farm,* as well as the critically acclaimed adult nonfiction book *Breaking the TV Habit.* A graduate of Yale University, she is a frequent speaker on women's issues and the role of media in our lives. In an effort to share what she learned from her year by the sea, she holds "Weekend by the Sea" seminars, which are designed to help women reacquaint themselves with their feminine heritage, explore the bare essentials in simple living, and learn the art of being present. She has appeared on the *Oprah Winfrey Show*, the *Saturday Today Show*, and numerous other broadcasts in connection with her bestselling books *A Year by the Sea* and *An Unfinished Marriage*. Anderson lives with her husband on Cape Cod. She welcomes letters and e-mails from readers. You may reach her at Box 1314, Harwich, MA 02645, or at joanleeand@webtv.net. She can also address your questions in her column at www.sistersforsisters.com.